THE HISTORY OF SAINT BONAVENTURE CHURCH

AND THE SURROUNDING AREA

BY DOLORIS KIRSCHBAUM

DEDICATED...

To Rev. Michael J. Murray who organized and coordinated the events of the 75th year; he gave the Book Committee carte blanche and never interfered.

SECRETARIAT OF STATE

No. 178780   FROM THE VATICAN, June 27, 1986

Dear Cardinal Bernardin,

    The Holy Father was pleased to be informed that Saint Bonaventure Parish in Chicago is celebrating the Seventy-fifth Anniversary of its establishment.

    On this joyful occasion His Holiness is united spiritually with all the members of the Parish. He gives thanks to the Lord for the graces bestowed on the parishioners over the past seventy-five years through the preaching of the word of God and through the sacramental ministry of the Church, especially through the Eucharistic Sacrifice, which in the expression of the Second Vatican Council remains "the source and summit of all Christian life" (<u>Lumen Gentium</u>, 11).

    The Holy Father prays that this commemoration will be for the whole community an occasion for renewed fervor in authentic Christian living, according to the standards of the Gospel.

    With these sentiments His Holiness sends his Apostolic Blessing, in pledge of joy and peace in Jesus Christ.

    With every personal good wish, I remain

                  Sincerely yours in Christ,

                    +E. Martínez
                    Substitute

Pope John Paul greeting Pastor, Michael Murray, in Vatican City

1555 North State Parkway
Chicago, Illinois 60610

June 17, 1986

Dear Friends in the Lord Jesus:

    On the occasion of the celebration of the Diamond Jubilee Year of Saint Bonaventure Parish, I wish to extend to you all my congratulations, best wishes and promise of prayers.

    Anniversaries are a time for celebrating the many persons who have preceded us and built a tradition of faith and love. Your anniversary is also a time to celebrate the present parishioners, supporters and friends of Saint Bonaventure Parish, and to ask for God's continued blessings in the future.

    As I shall be attending October meetings in Rome, I am regretfully unable to be with you in person. However, be assured that you will all be in my thoughts and prayers, -- especially on October 11th and 12th, which will mark the culminating ceremonies of this joyous Diamond Jubilee Year.

    With cordial good wishes, I remain

Sincerely yours in Christ,

Joseph Card. Bernardin
Archbishop of Chicago

Diamond Jubilee Celebration
Saint Bonaventure Parish
1911 - 1986

THE WHITE HOUSE

WASHINGTON

September 30, 1986

To the Congregation of
   Saint Bonaventure Church of Chicago:

Congratulations on your 75th anniversary. I know you must be very proud to have reached this milestone.

As a nation united under God, our best efforts are directed toward the achievement of that enduring peace which is founded on respect for the God-given worth and dignity of every human person. In this commitment, the work of America's religious institutions is more important than ever. The comfort, compassion and moral guidance traditionally provided by churches and synagogues continue to inspire men and women in their selfless pursuit of the common good. We Americans are a proud and patriotic people. But we have always recognized that we owe our first allegiance to the God Who has so generously endowed us, for it is by His blessings that we prosper.

Nancy joins me in sending warm best wishes for your celebration. May God continue to bless you in all your endeavors.

Ronald Reagan

STATE OF ILLINOIS
OFFICE OF THE GOVERNOR
SPRINGFIELD 62706

JAMES R. THOMPSON
GOVERNOR

October 11, 1986

Reverend Michael J. Murray, Pastor
Saint Bonaventure Rectory
1641 West Diversey Parkway
Chicago, Illinois 60614

Dear Father Murray:

As Governor of Illinois, it is my great pleasure to congratulate you and the parishoners of Saint Bonaventure on the Diamond Jubilee of your parish.

For the past 75 years, Saint Bonaventure has served the spiritual, educational and social needs of a growing Catholic community. It has provided a sense of unity and stability for the people of this community.

I commend the priests, sisters, teachers and many parishoners of Saint Bonaventure. Your hard work and dedication have made your parish the positive force that it is for the people of this area.

On behalf of the more than 11 1/2 million people of Illinois, please accept my sincere best wishes for a most enjoyable Diamond Jubilee Celebration.

Sincerely,

James R. Thompson
GOVERNOR

JRT/pm

DAN ROSTENKOWSKI
8TH DISTRICT, ILLINOIS

COMMITTEES:
CHAIRMAN
COMMITTEE ON
WAYS AND MEANS

CHAIRMAN
JOINT COMMITTEE ON
TAXATION

Congress of the United States
House of Representatives
Washington, D.C. 20515

November 13, 1986

Reverend Father Michael Murray
St. Bonaventure's Church
1641 West Diversey Avenue
Chicago, Illinois 60614

Dear Father Murray:

I want to take this opportunity to join you and all your parishioners in celebrating the 75th anniversary of Saint Bonaventure Parish. St. Bonaventure has become a landmark in the neighborhood offering spirtual comfort and merciful service to all in need.

St. Bonaventure has witnessed continuous growth and change during its 75 years. Through it all, it has remained an anchor in the neighborhood. As a church of immigrants, it first opened its doors to welcome the wave of Europeans during the early part of the century. Today, it continues in that role, extending its arms to new arrivals from all parts of the world.

The great contributions which St. Bonaventure has made throughout the years will long be remembered by those touched by its generosity. May you celebrate many more anniversaries.

With best wishes, I remain

Sincerely yours,

Dan Rostenkowski
Member of Congress

DR/pv

THERIS M. GABINSKI

ALDERMAN, 32ND WARD

2150 N. DAMEN AVENUE - 60647

TELEPHONE: CA 7-1100

CITY COUNCIL
CITY OF CHICAGO

COUNCIL CHAMBER
ROOM 304, CITY HALL
TELEPHONE: 744-6567

November 13, 1986

COMMITTEE MEMBERSHIPS

ZONING
(CHAIRMAN)

EMPLOYMENT
(VICE-CHAIRMAN)

ADMINISTRATION, REORGANIZATION AND PERSONNEL

CABLE TELEVISION

COMMITTEES AND RULES

FINANCE

HOUSING AND NEIGHBORHOOD DEVELOPMENT

HUMAN RIGHTS AND CONSUMER PROTECTION

NEIGHBORHOOD AND COMMUNITY AFFAIRS

SPECIAL EVENTS AND WORLD'S FAIR

Father Michael Murray
St. Bonaventure Parish
1641 West Diversey Avenue
Chicago, Illinois 60614

Dear Father Murray:

My warmest Congratulations on this occasion of your 75th Anniversary. You can well be proud of your parish and its service to the community.

You have won the respect, confidence and admiration of the people in this area and have every right to be proud of your accomplishments. We all owe you a debt of gratitude for your years of community service and the education of countless children.

I am sure that your parishioners have worked hard and sacrificed much to support St. Bonaventure Parish these past 75 years, my congratulations to them all.

With warmest wishes for the future, I am

Sincerely yours,

Terry Gabinski
Alderman, 32nd Ward

TG:ck

PAUL SIMON
ILLINOIS

COMMITTEES:
LABOR AND HUMAN RESOURCES
JUDICIARY
RULES AND ADMINISTRATION

United States Senate
WASHINGTON, DC 20510

September 19, 1986

Rev. Michael J. Murray
Saint Bonaventure Rectory
1641 W. Diversey Parkway
Chicago, Illinois 60614

Dear Rev. Murray:

Congratulations on the upcoming celebration of St. Bonaventure's Diamond anniversary.

I am sure that during seventy-five years your parish has served thousands of Chicagoans develop their religous and community spirits.

I am proud to join your community in congratulating you on this special occasion and want to wish you the very best for the future.

If I can be of assistance to you in any way, please let me know.

My best wishes.

Cordially,

Paul Simon
U.S. Senator

230 S. Dearborn (3892)
Chicago, Illinois 60604
(312) 353-4952

PS/jk

---

230 S. DEARBORN
KLUCZYNSKI BLDG., 38TH FLOOR
CHICAGO, IL 60604
312/353-4952

3 WEST OLD CAPITOL PLAZA
SUITE 1
SPRINGFIELD, IL 62701
217/492-4960

8787 STATE ST.
SUITE 212
EAST ST. LOUIS, IL 62203
618/398-7707

250 WEST CHERRY
ROOM 115-B
CARBONDALE, IL 62901
618/457-3653

SIDNEY R. YATES
9TH DISTRICT ILLINOIS

COMMITTEE
APPROPRIATIONS

CHAIRMAN, INTERIOR AND
RELATED AGENCIES

Congress of the United States
House of Representatives
Washington, DC 20515-1309

WASHINGTON OFFICE:
2234 RAYBURN HOUSE OFFICE BUILDING
20515-1309
(202) 225-2111

DISTRICT OFFICES:
230 S DEARBORN STREET
CHICAGO, IL 60604-1663
(312) 353-4596

2100 RIDGE AVENUE
EVANSTON, IL 60204-2716
(312) 328-2610

October 7, 1986

Saint Bonaventure Church
1641 West Diversey Parkway
Chicago, Illinois 60614

Dear Friends:

I am delighted to have this opportunity to extend to all of you my warmest personal greetings on the very happy occasion of the 75th anniversary of St. Bonaventure Parish.

Saint Bonaventure has been a vital force in the community for 75 years and there is every reason to celebrate. What a splendid record of achievement and service you have. I know that the reunions and ceremonies that begin this Diamond Jubilee celebration will be a memorable event for everyone and a truly historic event in the history of the parish.

I want all of you to know that I am very honored to represent the people of St. Bonaventure Parish in the United States Congress. I congratulate you and wish you every happiness on this wonderful anniversary.

With kindest regards,

Sincerely yours,

SIDNEY R. YATES
Member of Congress

OFFICE OF THE MAYOR

CITY OF CHICAGO

HAROLD WASHINGTON
MAYOR

August 16, 1986

Dear Friends:

I am pleased to extend my greetings and best wishes to the Saint Bonaventure Catholic Church on this 75th Anniversary occasion. The service you have rendered to our Lord and to our community these many years has been most commendable and a true source of strength and inspiration.

It is always nice to know that there are ministers and their congregations who realize their goals. I am confident that this Diamond Jubilee Celebration is just one of many blessings to come.

Once again, congratulations to you and your congregation and best wishes for continued success in the future.

With warmest personal regards.

Sincerely,

Harold Washington
Mayor

Saint Bonaventure Catholic Church
1641 West Diversy Parkway
Chicago, Illinois 60614

MARTIN J. OBERMAN

ALDERMAN, 43RD WARD

2258 N. ORCHARD STREET - 60614

TELEPHONE: 472-0705

CITY COUNCIL
CITY OF CHICAGO

COUNCIL CHAMBER
SECOND FLOOR, CITY HALL

COMMITTEE MEMBERSHIPS

PUBLIC RECORDS AND INFORMATION
(CHAIRMAN)

ALCOHOLISM AND SUBSTANCE ABUSE

CULTURAL DEVELOPMENT AND HISTORICAL
LANDMARK PRESERVATION

EDUCATION

FINANCE

HOUSING AND NEIGHBORHOOD
DEVELOPMENT

LAND ACQUISITION AND DISPOSITION

LEASES

PUBLIC UTILITIES

TRAFFIC CONTROL AND SAFETY

To St. Bonaventure Parish:

    Congratulations on your Diamond Jubilee! St. Bonaventure has long been a strong community presence, rich in the cultures of different lands, and strong in the spiritual bonds of its peoples. For seventy-five years, your Parish has grown and flourished, and has truly been an asset to the area.

    I wish you, your family and your friends a truly joyous celebration, and many more wonderful and prosperous years

Sincerely,

Martin J. Oberman
Alderman, 43rd Ward

FOREWORD

In our efforts to do a comprehensive study of the history of St. Bonaventure and the surrounding area, certain records and documents crucial to the accuracy of the early history are no longer available and we have had to rely upon the memories of many of our parishioners, former and present parish priests and the Sisters of St. Joseph. With their assistance we have pieced together and cross-checked the information we have obtained.

We would like to take this opportunity to thank all those who took time to contribute information to our search — they made this book possible.

Within the time allotted, we believe we have succeeded in compiling an accurate history — in all respects possible — to the development of St. Bonaventure and the surrounding neighborhood since —

PREFACE

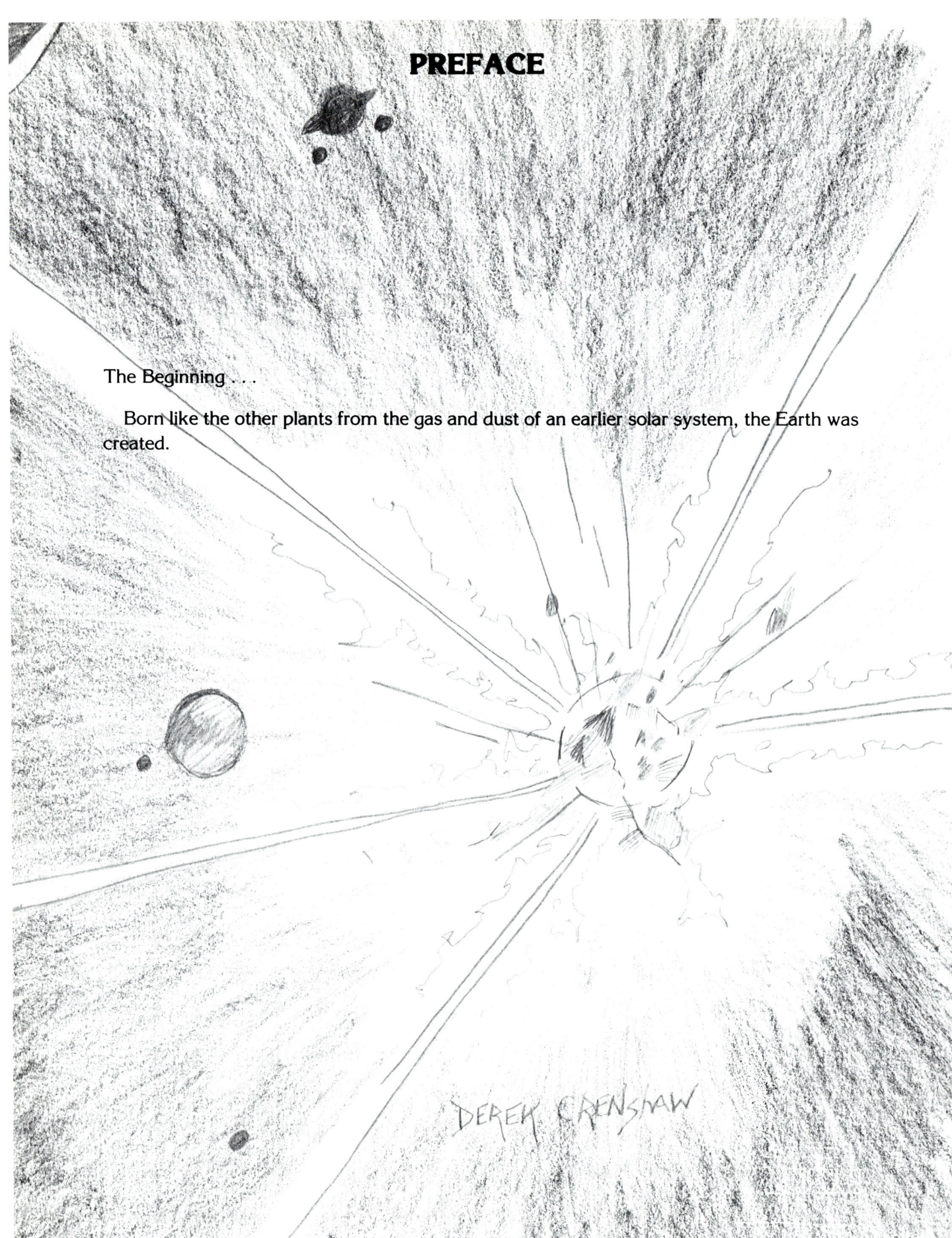

The Beginning . . .

Born like the other plants from the gas and dust of an earlier solar system, the Earth was created.

As the surface of the Earth cooled into a solid crust, organisms evolved, then soft-bodied creatures, plants, early reptiles and for the next 140 million years the great dinosaurs and mammals inhabited the Earth. Suddenly, many of Earth's inhabitants became extinct from forces no one can positively identify.

The first ice age occurred, perhaps two and one-half billion years ago, followed by successive great periods of ice lasting millions of years. During the last ice age, however, ice sheets covering large parts of Europe, North America and South America made important alterations in the terrain of the glaciated regions; leveling sections and eroding hollows that would later become lakes — The Great Lakes — then flooding the lakes in their wake.

Within the last million years, flowering plants, insects and mammals appeared once again.

Man

emerged

in

North

America

some

48,000

years

ago.

As early as the sixth century the Great Lakes Basin was inhabited by ancestors of the North American Indians — the Mound Builders — whose extensive earthwork can be found today in this area. Meanwhile, Europe and Asia were being civilized and tamed.

By the 1400's, the Fox, the Illini, the Ojibwa, the Ottawa, the Pottawattomie, the Sac and the Winnebago Indians were living and working on the land of the Great Lakes region. As will be evident later, the long struggle between the expanding European population and the Indian would soon begin.

1674-75, Louis Joliet, a French adventurer, and Father Marquette, a Jesuit Chaplain, were the first explorers to explore the future site of Chicago; they were followed by LaSalle who reached the mouth of the Chicago River April 9, 1692, and claimed the region for France.

The Great Lakes Basin was an integral part of the Old Northwest that came within the United States boundaries by the Treaty of Paris of September 3, 1783, thereby ending the American Revolution. Under the ordinance of 1787 the area became the Northwest Territory — the first possession of the United States.

Fort Dearborn was established in 1803 at the mouth of the Chicago River. When the war of 1812 was declared on June 18th, the Pottawattomie, siding with the British, attacked the fort the morning of August 15, 1812 killing soldiers and civilians. The next day the fort was destroyed by fire. Confidence was later restored, Fort Dearborn was rebuilt in 1816 and the Enabling Act of 1818 conferred statehood on the Illinois Territory.

The opening of the Erie Canal in 1825 provided a

water route from the eastern seaboard to the site of Chicago. The first white settlers were already established and the population started to escalate, the land was being cleared and homes and farms were being built. The Black Hawk War (1832) practically ended the tenure of the Indian in Illinois. By about 1850, as the population grew, commerce and industry developed.

Lake View was incorporated as a town February 16, 1865.

THE SURROUNDING AREA

H.J. Lucas, President of Northwestern Terra Cotta Works standing next to terra cotta vase.

Northwestern Terra Cotta Works — statue of Christ the King.

Northwestern Terra Cotta Works

By about 1870, the Lake View area already had a reputation as the center of the terra cotta (Latin for "burnt earth") industry in this country. At the corner of Diversey Parkway and Ashland Avenue, Louis Reimer and Augusta Kuester established the Reimer-Kuester Brick Manufacturing Company. At Altgeld and Wrightwood Avenues the original Chicago Terra Cotta Company, one of the few commercial concerns to escape the great fire in 1871, was already producing bricks to meet the needs of the fast growing community and to help rebuild the city after the catastrophe. These were only two of many brick manufacturers in the Lake View area.

In 1878 the Chicago Terra Cotta Company was succeeded by the Northwestern Terra Cotta Works. Also in 1878, the Northwestern Terra Cotta Works procured their clay from what is now the site of St. Bonaventure and also from a clay hole at Greenview and Diversey. At this period in time, they produced mainly bricks, flower pots, vases, etc.

Eventually, the clay pits were depleted and abandoned in this area. The Northwestern Terra Cotta Works then began importing clay by the car load from a site in Ohio.

Sanford Loring, the company's treasurer and practicing architect turned the Northwestern Terra Cotta Works from brick producers into creators of archi-

tectural terra cotta.

Elmer Landini who worked numerous years at Northwestern Terra Cotta Works relates how the clay was turned into "objet d'art."

Sand and pulverized terra cotta were added to the clay; after grinding this mixture to a powder, water was added. The clay was then pressed into molds, and after stiffening, removed from the molds and allowed to dry. After drying, they were sprayed with a liquid glaze, and then the clay objects were started through a tunnel kiln the length of the building for firing. As they moved through the kiln the temperature was gradually raised to approximately 2000 degrees Fahrenheit. The terra cotta objects would get "white hot" as they approached the middle of the tunnel and would be gradually cooled as they neared the end. This baking process took approximately one week to complete. After they came out they were again sprayed with a liquid glaze, which during another subsequent firing, developed into a protective cover.

A terra cotta cornice made by the Chicago Terra Cotta Company can be seen on the Old Capital building in Springfield, Illinois.

The Northwestern Terra Cotta Works furnished ornamental architectural terra cotta for many renowned buildings throughout the United States and some notable examples here in Chicago namely: the Rookery Building, 209 South LaSalle; the Railway Exchange Building, 80 East Jackson; The Wrigley Building, 410 North Michigan; The Blackstone Hotel, 636 South Michigan; the Merchandise Mart; the Carbide and Carbon Building, 230 North Michigan; the Chicago Theater, 175 North States Street; the Chicago Board of Trade, 141 West Jackson; the Manhattan Building, 423-39 South Dearborn; St. Thomas the Apostle School, 5467 South Woodlawn; the Reliance Building, 32 North State Street; the Fisher Building, 343 South Dearborn; the Germania Club Building, Clark and North Avenue; the Troescher Building, South Market Street; the Rialto Theater, 14 West Van Buren; the Tree Studio, East Ohio Street; and the Reebie Storage Building which is considered Egyptian Art Deco, fashioned after King Tutankhamen's egyptian motif.

During their peak production years, Northwestern Terra Cotta employed an average of 2,700 people at one time. They went out of business in 1957.

The Deering Works of International Harvester —

William Deering, founder of the Deering Harvester Company in Plano, Illinois in 1879, moved to the Chicago area and established the James Deering Harvester Machine Plant. James Deering was the son of William Deering. The site bounded by Fullerton and Clybourn avenues, Leavitt Street and the north branch of the Chicago River began producing primarily twine binders, and twine and rolling mills. In 1902 Deering Harvester Company was one of the principal companies to merge with McCormick Harvester Machine Company — Cyrus Hall McCormick, inventor of the reaper — and three other companies to form the International Harvester Company.

At full capacity, the Deering Works covered a land area of eighty acres. Literally a city itself; with streets and avenues between structures and several locomotives transporting materials or finished machines on miles of track which wound about through the plant, an electrical power house, miles of telephone wire and the best equipped private fire department in America.

At their peak they employed an average of 7,000 people, and had an annual capacity for turning out approximately 300,000 various farm and industrial machines. Their twine mills alone turned out 45,000 tons of twine each year.

During the summer of 1934, fire all but leveled the James Deering Works. Consequently, International Harvester started disposing of the property, part of which was to become the Julia Lathrop Homes, and in 1946 they announced the sale of the last of the property for development and resale into smaller parcels.

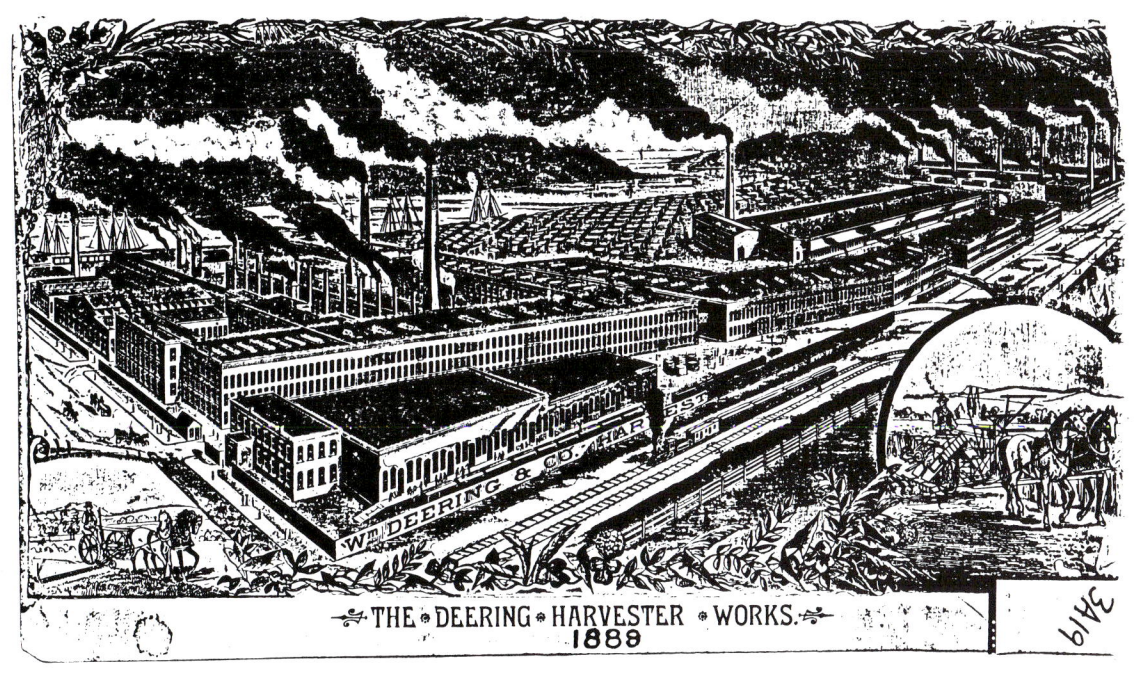

THE DEERING HARVESTER WORKS.
1889

"Boiling Cauldron Murder Case"

Shortly after the great fire a german emigrant, Adolph Louis Luetgert, arrived in Chicago to make his fortune. Uneducated and after following various occupations, he opened a grocery store and saloon at Clybourn and Webster Avenues. In 1877, Mr. Luetgert's wife died leaving an infant son, and not long after he sold the saloon and opened a small sausage factory. He married again to Louisa Beckenese and devoted his energies to his sausage business which was growing and fast becoming well known.

Producing approximately three million pounds of sausage a year, Mr. Luetgert wanted to be sausage king of the world, and with two investors, he set about to expand his empire but greatly overextended his resources. In 1894 he purchased a new five story plant at the corner of 1501 Hermitage and Diversey (currently the 1700 block of Diversey) and named it the A.L. Luetgert Sausage Works.

All the while Mr. Luetgert was acquiring a reputation as a womanizer.

By the early part of the 1897, swindled out his property and his factory temporarily closed down, his empire was collapsing and his wife's constant nagging was leading to violent confrontations.

It was learned later that on March 11th, Adolph Luetgert accepted delivery at the plant of 300 pounds of crude potash and 50 pounds of arsenic.

On the night of May 1st, Mrs. Luetgert was observed walking toward the sausage plant with Adolph — never to be seen again.

The night watchman, Frank Bialk, was sent away on an errand and was told to go home for the rest of the evening. The next morning he returned to find Mr. Luetgert asleep at a desk and noted a sausage vat was overflowing with a greasy substance bubbling over on the floor.

Louisa's brother, Diederick Beckenese, came to the city on May 4th to call on his sister. Learning his sister had been missing since the previous Saturday night and soon discovering her personal affects were still intact, Diederick went to the Sheiffield Avenue police station and reported the matter to the police. The

police, not suspecting foul play, had area clay holes and the river dragged. Mr. Luetgert was absolutely indifferent, not making one inquiry in the police progress.

The police discovering nothing, questioned the night watchman and other employees of the factory. They were told of the events of the evening of May 1st and, in particular the story surrounding the bubbling vat.

After a thorough search of the factory, Police found two rings near the corner of the suspect vat; a plain gold ring and small ring which was sometimes used as a guard of friendship ring; upon examination they found inside the letters L.L. engraved. (The ring was identified as belonging to Louisa.) Also in the vat they found a small piece of bone.

Examination of debris dumped on Hermitage from the factory revealed more bone fragments, a false tooth, a corset stay and upon an inspection of Mr. Luetgert's private quarters in the plant, they found dark stains resembling blood on the walls.

On May 17th Mr. Luetgert was arrested for murder.

Adolph Luetgert was indicted and subsequently went to trial August 23rd where the State's Attorney, Charles Deneen, called Mr. Luetgert an "inhuman fiend" who sat by and watched his wife's body disintegrate in the bubbling vat.

The greatest problem was proving Louisa had been murdered — there was no body.

Speculation of what might have happened to Louisa caused all sausage sales to drastically drop, and to be sure the story didn't die neighborhood children chanted while jumping rope.

"Old man Luetgert made sausage out of his wife.
He turned on the steam.
His wife began to scream.
There'll be a hot time in the old town tonight."

The trial lasted two months when the case was turned over to the jury. After 38 hours of balloting, nine jurors were for conviction, three for acquittal.

A second trial started December 15, 1897 after jury selection. Again the dominant question of 'where was the body?' was the key to guilt or innocence. Except this time, Dr. G. A. Dorsey, anthropologist and curator at the Field Museum testified after examining the bone fragments that they were human.

Mr. Luetgert, in order to refute damaging testimony, took the stand to tell his version of what happened that night. His reason for the mixture in the vat, "I was making soap." He also claimed Louisa wandered away from home while demented.

On February 9, 1898 the jurors agreed and found Mr. Luetgert guilty; because there was no body they sentenced him to life in prison rather than hanging.

Adolph Luetgert was taken to Joliet prison. He died 18 months later on July 27, 1899 of heart failure. In 1902 the sausage factory caught fire and burned to the ground.

Far left: Adolph Luetgert [top] and his wife, Louisa [in drawings from the front page of the Chicago Times-Herald of 1897], and the sausage factory on the Northwest Side that the immigrant German tanner opened in 1894.

> By about 1885, the land at Diversey and Ashland was sold and was being filled. Around 1890, the land was sub-divided and split into lots. Lots 23, 24, 25, 26 and 27 (the future site of St. Bonaventure Church) were sold to a Miss Anna Cassidy.
>
> Today, not quite one-hundred years later, if you stand on the north side of Diversey and look south down Marshfield just past St. Bonaventure Church, and with a little imagination, you can see the outline of the clay pit.

Stewart-Warner Corporation

The year 1897 is generally accepted as the company's birth date. In that year John K. Stewart and Thomas Jefferson Clark incorporated their Chicago Flexible Shaft Company. In 1905 they formed Stewart and Clark Manufacturing Company and erected a small plant building on West Diversey Parkway to produce speedometers.

The new corporation achieved very rapid success.

Almost concurrently with Stewart and Clark's entrance into the speedometer business the Warner Instrument Company was formed at Beloit, Wisconsin to manufacture portable tachometers.

In 1912, prior to a settlement of patent litigations, Stewart and Clark Manufacturing Company and Warner Instrument Company were consolidated by formation of a new corporation, which was called Stewart-Warner Speedometer Corporation, and shares were offered to the public for the first time. Warner's tachometer production was then moved to the Chicago plant.

In July 1907 Mr. Clark was killed demonstrating a Stewart speedometer in a Packard automobile. He was only thirty-eight. Mr. J.K. Stewart died suddenly, at the age of forty-five, in June 1916. Mrs. Stewart died nine months after her husband, leaving two daughters and a complicated guardianship and estate litigation to be sorted out by the courts that gained national prominence in the nation's press.

Mr. C.B. Smith then became president and chief executive officer of Stewart-Warner Speedometer and seemed intent upon a program of rapid expansion. Through a series of acquisitions Stewart-Warner's position as the largest manufacturer in the motorcycle instrument market and passenger car industry was unquestioned.

One other accomplishment that proved to be C.B. Smith's greatest success was the purchase of the Bassick-Alemite Corporation in 1925. Further in 1925 he had entered them in the new rapidly-growing radio field.

In April 1929, the name of the company was changed to Stewart-Warner Corporation.

In 1933 after a bitter proxy fight, with charges of nepotism, mismanagement and contractual disputes, there followed a barrage of charges and counter-charges which resulted in postponing the annual stockholders meeting and thereafter Mr. Smith presented his resignation. Early in 1934 Mr. James S. Knowlson took over as president.

The years 1940 through 1945 and again during the Korean War were marked by the rapid and almost complete conversion of Stewart-Warner's business to military production.

Early in 1954, with Mr. Knowlson's concurrence, the board of directors agreed to bring into the corporation a new president and chief executive officer, Mr. Bennett Archambault.

Stewart-Warner's business is largely automotive — and today has the distinction of being the largest manufacturer on the north side of Chicago, employing over 2,500 people.

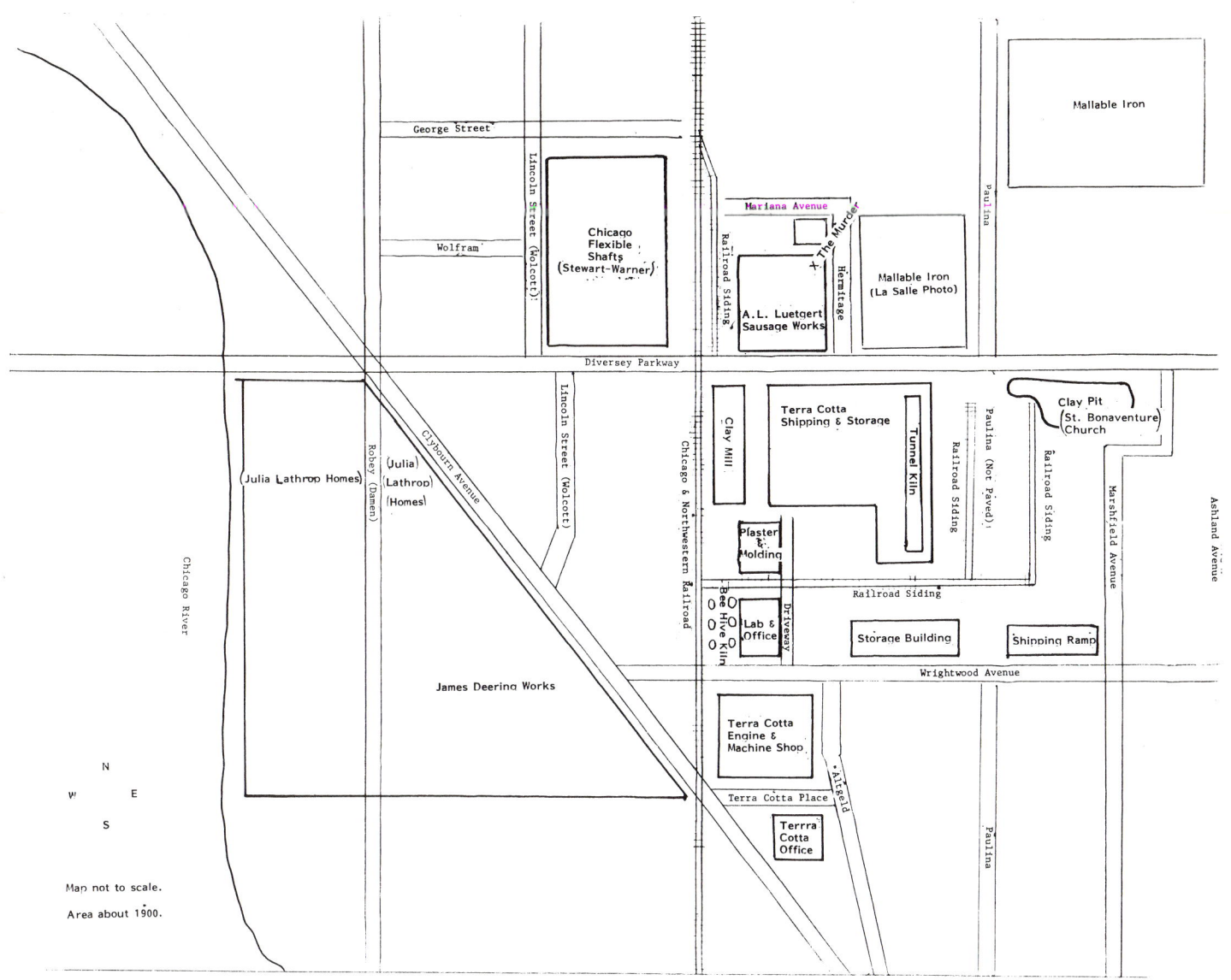

Ash Manor

One of St. Bonaventure's neighbors that cannot be overlooked, is the interesting old house at 1600 Diversey, now the elegant and famous Ash Manor Restaurant. It was originally constructed in 1907 as a private residence of William E. Schlake and his family. At the time, Mr. Schlake was president of Illinois Brick Company, member of the Illinois Racing Commission and prominent local politician. He and his family resided in the home for over thirty years.

Doctor Alex J.G. Friend, MD. Ph.D. then took over the house and turned it into his medical offices and a mini hospital until the mid 1970's. Dr. Friend died November 10, 1981.

In 1979, vacant and in need of major repair, the building was acquired by Frank DeBartolo, a Chicago-area businessman. After a time of planning and extensive restoration, the house was returned to its turn-of-the century splendor.

On January 11, 1911, Miss Cassidy sold to the Catholic Bishop of Chicago the five lots for $12,000.00.

SAINT BONAVENTURE PARISH

St. Bonaventure Church

The reality of jobs at Northwestern Terra Cotta Works, the Deering Works of International Harvester and Stewart-Warner Corporation attracted many immigrant workers, farmers, skilled tradesmen and the like to the growing Lake View Community. In 1910 Rev. Henry Willis was commissioned to survey the large area between the parishes of St. Andrew and St. Vincent Depaul for the purpose of establishing an English speaking parish; St. Alphonsus was German speaking and St. Josaphat, Polish-Kashubian. Advising him were some of St. Bonaventure's future parishioners; Dennis S. Ryan, James C. Smith and Clinton Uller among others. It seemed feasible, therefore, to place the new church of St. Bonaventure near Diversey Parkway and Ashland Avenue. A proposed site at Wellington and Damen Avenues was rejected because of proximity to St. Andrew's Church.

When the parish was officially established on October 11, 1911, Ty Cobb of the Detroit Tigers (American League) and Frank Schulte of Chicago's Cubs (National League) were named most valuable players of their respective leagues.

In the infant stages of the parish, Mass was offered first at the Schneider public school and later in a neighborhood hall at Diversey and Paulina.

Concurrent with the construction of the church (1911-12), the States of New Mexico and Arizona joined the Union; the Titanic struck an iceberg and sank in the North Atlantic; Jim Thorpe won the decathlon and the pentathlon at the 1912 Olympics held in Stockholm, Sweden and William Howard Taft was president of the United States.

Built in Romanesque style the church is 125 feet by 65 feet. The Architect, Joseph Mollitor; Mason, Van Etten; Carpenter, L. Baleb.

Saint Bonaventure

The Church was named for Saint Bonaventure who was born in 1217 at Bagnorea, Italy. He was named John. During an illness as an infant, St. Francis of Assisi miraculously cured the infant and exclaimed "Buona Venture" (meaning good things to come, a child of benediction). From that time on he was known as Bonaventure. Bonaventure entered the Franciscan Order at the age of 17, and about 1241 went to Paris to pursue theological studies. At the University of Paris, he became acquainted with Thomas Acquinas, a friendship that lasted through life (both dying in the same year). On one occasion Thomas inquired of Bonaventure where he had obtained all his knowledge. He replied: "from my library." Thomas asked to see his Library. Bonaventure showed him the crucifix. In 1257, at age 36, Bonaventure was chosen General of his Order.

In those days, the leading textbook in Sacred Theology was the Book of Sentences written by Peter Lombard about the year 1140. Bonaventure wrote four volumes on the Sentences and lectured on the Gospels and the Creation.

After the founder, St. Francis of Assisi, Bonaventure was without doubt the greatest Father General the Order ever had.

After his appointment as Archbishop of York, Pope Clement IV, who had been appointed to England before his election to the papacy was not permitted by the English to set foot on their soil. After his election as Pope, he strove to find a man who would measure up in the difficult ecclesiastical affairs of England; he wrote to Bonaventure that he was that man. Bonaventure pleaded not to be sent and the Pope yielded. If Bonaventure had gone, England might not have fallen away from the faith later.

In 1273 Pope Gregory X consecrated Bonaventure Cardinal and Bishop of Albaon. When the envoys came to the monastery with the Red Hat, Bonaventure was working in the kitchen washing dishes. He told them to hang "the hat" on the clothes tree until he had completed his task.

Perhaps the greatest mystical Theologian of the middle ages, he was also famous for writing many sermons and commentaries on Holy Scripture, as well as a "Life" of the founder of his order. He died the night of July 15, 1274. He is buried in Lyons, France.

St. Bonaventure was canonized by Sixtus IV in 1482. A century later he was declared a Doctor of the Church by Pope Sixtus V.

The Church Building

The corner store was laid by Bishop Rhode on August 18, 1912, but construction did not proceed smoothly. As the church was near completion there was a work stoppage which lasted almost a year, during this period the floor remained unfinished. Nevertheless, George Seebacher was the first baby baptized in the church on December 8, 1912, but Ray Ferguson was the first child baptized in the parish (before the church was completed).

Frank Daniels recalls about 1911, the same time the church was being built, the Ashland Avenue street car line was being installed, but it only ran as far as Fullerton Avenue on the south end since there was no bridge at that time. Shortly thereafter the sidewalks made of "wooden blocks" were being changed to concrete.

The east wall of the church goes down eight feet into the ground, but the west wall is sunk sixteen feet under the ground because the edge of the clayhole began about the middle of the church. Virginia Abbott, a long-time parishioner, remembers while the church was being constructed, the neighborhood children would naturally start playing around the construction site. Fr. Peter Geraghty wanting to discourage this practice would start by yelling and then chasing kids who would run across the street, where the convent is today, and hide in giant sunflowers that were planted at that time. The gym, originally the old hall, was planned and built with the church containing an assembly hall, coal bin and boiler room.

Rev. Martin J. McGuire was appointed as its first pastor. "Peeler" (so called from Sir Robert Peel, organizer of the Irish constabulary) McGuire was a constable in Ireland before coming to the United States and entering the priesthood. He was ordained in St. Louis in 1901.

The parish increased so as to demand an assistant priest and Rev. Peter Gereghty was appointed to help Fr. McGuire until 1917 when he was succeeded by Fr. Peter Quinn. In 1926 Rev. Henry Weber was appointed assistant but remained for only a short time.

As a matter of incidental interest, during the late 1920's Diversey Parkway was under the control of the Park District Police rather than the Chicago Police as it is today, and Park District headquarters were located next to the Zoo in Lincoln Park.

The house at 1615 Diversey — originally the office of the Reimer-Keuster Brick Manufacturing Company was moved from across the street — became the rectory.

Rev. Martin J. McGuire, founding pastor of St. Bonaventure

Left to Right: Standing: Mary McKenna and Margaret Hill. Sitting: Joseph Hill and James Cavanaugh. Double wedding ceremony at St. Bonaventure on November 27, 1912.

Standing Left to Right: Jack Whelan and Dennis Ryan; sitting Margaret O'Connor and Mary Ellen (O'Connor) Ryan — Married at St. Bonaventure Sept. 22, 1915. Dennis Ryan was a charter member of St. Bonnie's.

Paul and Tillie Battiste — First Communion 1912.

1914 — Confirmation Day for Susan and George Pellicore.

Mamie Blaul and the Sullivan girls — 1917.

Sisters of St. Joseph

The Sisters of St. Joseph under the direction of Sister Patricia, principal, and her assistants; Srs. Austin, Desales, Gilberta, Adelbert, Philomene and Edward, opened the parish school in 1913. There was no housing available for the sisters when they arrived; seven nuns occupied two rooms over the church. Then the house at 1618 Diversey was rented for the next two years until the convent was built. St. Bonaventure was the first school within the city limits to be staffed by the Sisters. The Congregation of the Sisters of St. Joseph originated in LePuy, France in 1650. Their order was established in St. Louis (1836) and branched to LaGrange, Illinois in 1899 where it is today. Eighteen girls from the parish became Sisters of St. Joseph; also seven others joined other religious orders to date.

Sisters at St. Bonaventure 1939-40 Virginia, Margaret, Roberta, Dolores, Loyola, Ethelreda, Christina, Jane Frances, Alms, Madeline, Alberta, Agatha

RELIGIOUS WHO TAUGHT AT SAINT BONAVENTURE

1921	Sr. M. Regina	1933	Sr. M. Brendan		Sr. M. Roberta
	Sr. M. Sacred Heart		Sr. M. Linus		Sr. M. Jane Frances
	Sr. M. Berchmans		Sr. M. Dorothy		Sr. M. Margaret
	Sr. M. Liguori		Sr. M. Alberta	1940	Sr. M. Clare
	Sr. M. Gerard	1934	Sr. M. Loyola		Sr. M. Joanne
	Sr. M. Eucharista		Sr. M. Oliver		Sr. M. Constance
1926	Sr. M. Fidelis		Sr. Joan Marie		Sr. M. Augustine
1928	Sr. M. Ambrose		Sr. M. Petronilla	1941	Sr. M. Wilma
	Sr. M. Daniel	1935	Sr. M. Norbert		Sr. M. Constance
	Sr. M. Elizabeth	1936	Sr. M. David		Sr. Miriam Therese
1929	Sr. M. Gabriel		Sr. M. Camilla	1942	Sr. Dominic
1930	Sr. M. Aquinas	1937	Sr. M. Genevieve		Sr. Antonia
	Sr. M. Angela	1938	Sr. M. Madeline		Sr. Laura Annette
1931	Sr. M. Francis		Sr. M. Austin	1943	Sr. Lawrence James
	Sr. M. Stella		Sr. M. Ethelreda		Sr. Bernice
	Sr. M. Christina		Sr. M. Margaret		Sr. Michael Ann
	Sr. M. Good Shepherd	1939	Sr. M. Dolores		Sr. Nicholas
1932	Sr. M. Evangelista		Sr. M. Agatha	1944	Sr. Aquinata
	Sr. M. Francis Xavier		Sr. M. Madeline		Sr. Austin
	Sr. M. Carmelita		Sr. M. Alma		Sr. Eileen Marie
	Sr. M. Alfred		Sr. M. Virginia		Sr. Charles Ann

	Sr. Leonard		Sr. Maurita		Sr. Michael
1945	Sr. Kathleen Edward		Sr. Augustine		Sr. Margaret Flaherty
	Sr. Stanislaus		Sr. Jarlath	1964	Sr. Samuel
	Sr. Joseph		Sr. Dennis Michael		Sr. Grace
1946	Sr. Perpetua	1953	Sr. Mercedes		Sr. Nora
	Sr. Jane Margaret		Sr. Linus		Sr. Collette Marie
	Sr. Marie Clarice		Sr. DeNeri		Sr. Gerard
	Sr. Sebastian		Sr. Florita	1965	Sr. Patrick Marie
1947	Sr. Irma Joseph	1954	Sr. Pauline		Sr. Gabriel
	Sr. Ignatius		Sr. Fidelis		Sr. Jerome
	Sr. George Agnes	1955	Sr. Agnesetta	1966	Sr. Charlotte Marie
	Sr. Marguerite		Sr. Christina		Sr. Hilary
	Sr. Marcella		Sr. Thomas Agnes	1967	Sr. Mark
	Sr. Jeanette	1957	Sr. Rosalie Carmel		Sr. Paula
	Sr. Henrietta		Sr. Evelyn		Sr. Rita Esposito
1948	Sr. Daniel		Sr. Irene		Sr. Joel
	Sr. Monica	1958	Sr. Rose		Sr. Mariettina
	Sr. Domitilla		Sr. Maureen Francis	1968	Sr. Janet Daniels
1949	Sr. Edwardetta	1959	Sr. Charles		Sr. Sylvia Parkes
	Sr. Genevieve		Sr. Good Councel		Sr. Margaret Reynolds
	Sr. Kevin		Sr. Annamarie		Sr. Geraldine Ziak
	Sr. Dolorita		Sr. Raymond		Sr. Valeria
	Sr. Agnes		Sr. Bernadette		Sr. Pamela Bjurstrom
1950	Sr. Modesta		Sr. Pierre		Sr. Geraldine Shananhan
	Sr. Norine	1960	Sr. Ruth	1969	Sr. Diane Musial
	Sr. Frederick		Sr. Mildred		Sr. Therese Marczyk
	Sr. Benedicta		Sr. Donna Marie		Sr. Patricia Borchardt
	Sr. Rosaria		Sr. Kenneth	1970	Sr. Irene
1951	Sr. Clare	1961	Sr. Rene		Sr. Alice Vincent
	Sr. Francis		Sr. Robert Marie	1971	Sr. Marilyn Karlinski
	Sr. Rose		Sr. Roman		Sr. Dolores Lynch
	Sr. Patrick Marie	1962	Sr. Catherine	1972	Sr. Christine Myskow
	Sr. Margaret		Sr. Anita Therese		Sr. Margaret Parker
1952	Sr. John Edwin		Sr. Ursula		Sr. Lorraine Welker
	Sr. Edward Alishia	1963	Sr. Martin	1973	Sr. Sue Torgersen
	Sr. Veronica		Sr. Ronald		Bro. George Kolla
					Bro. William Easton
				1984	Sr. Mary Ann Boes, C.S.J.
					Sr. Mary Ann Budha, O.P.

Sister Bonaventure (Kathleen Hill) was the first girl from St. Bonaventure to enter the convent. She taught at the school before entering the convent but never returned to teach as a nun.

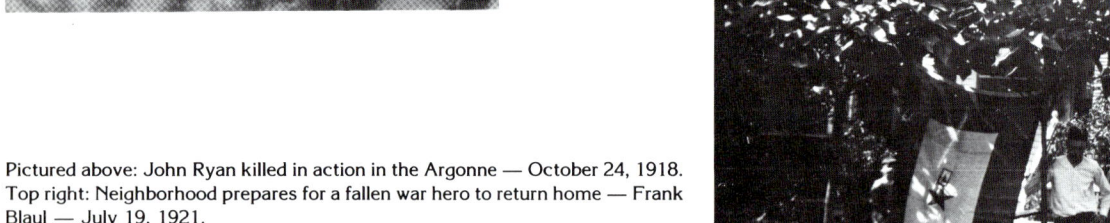

Pictured above: John Ryan killed in action in the Argonne — October 24, 1918.
Top right: Neighborhood prepares for a fallen war hero to return home — Frank Blaul — July 19, 1921.
Middle right: Neighbors await for remains of Frank Blaul to be returned home.
Bottom right: Frank Blaul — killed in action at Chateau Thierry — 1918.

World War I

"The Great War" — 1914-1918 — church records of parishioners who served during the War were never available. However, two men from St. Bonaventure were killed in action:

John Ryan who lived at 1750 Fletcher Street served at Headquarters Co. 353rd Infantry, 89th Division was killed October 24th, 1918 in the Argonne. Buried in France.

Frank Blaul who lived at 1938 Wolfman served in Co. B, 168th Infantry, 42nd (Rainbow) Division, died August 5th, 1918 of wounds received at Chateau Thierry. Buried in France. Later his remains were brought back to the United States and buried from St. Bonaventure.

Ashland Avenue
Alley
Marshfield
Clayhole
Church
Convent
School
School
Paulina Street
S
N
Diversey Parkway

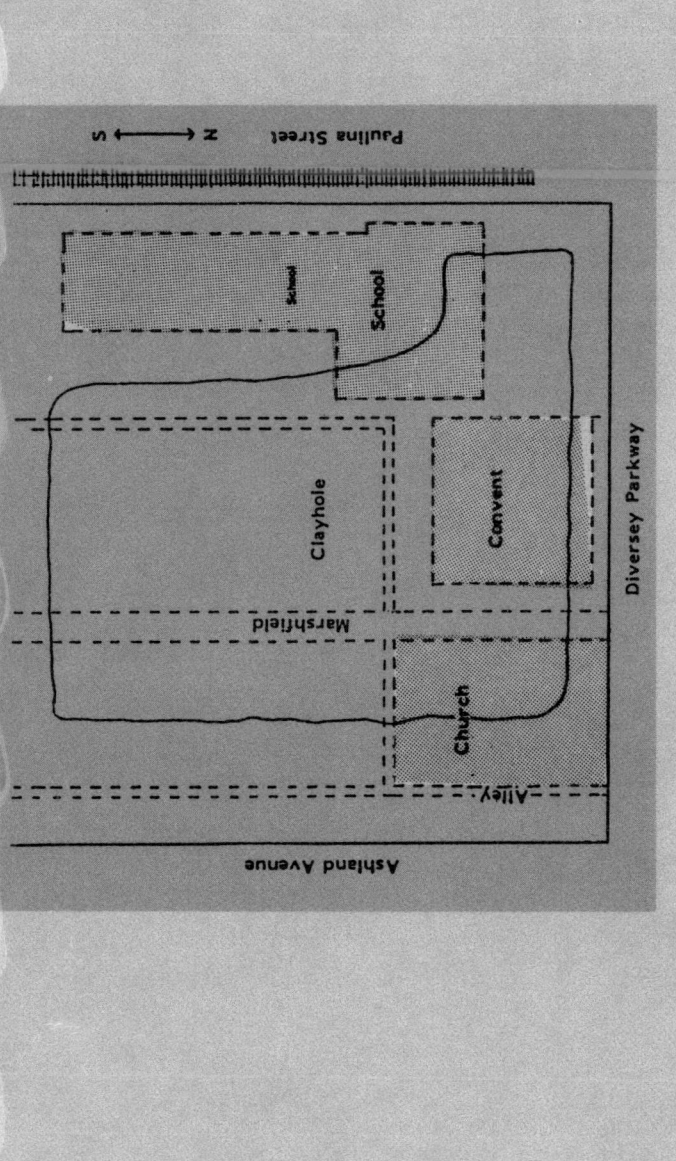

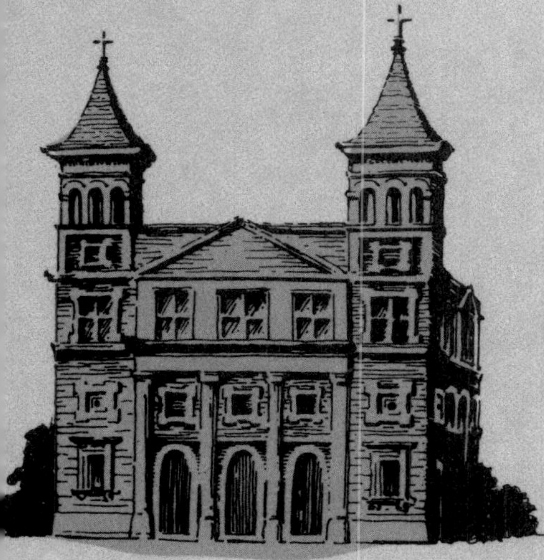

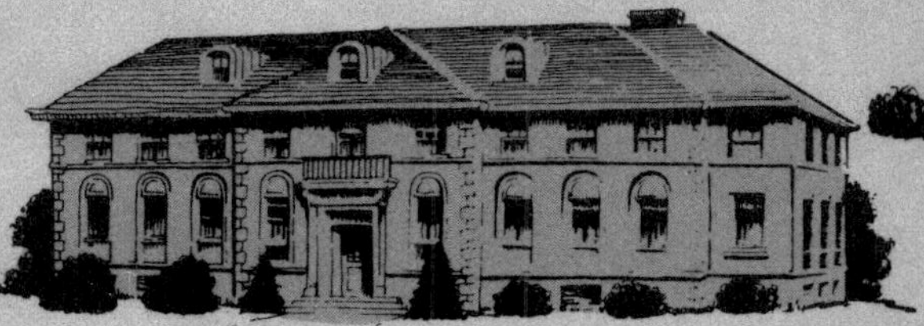

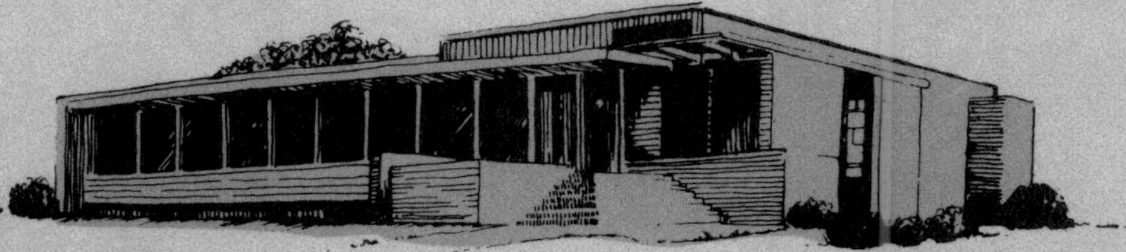

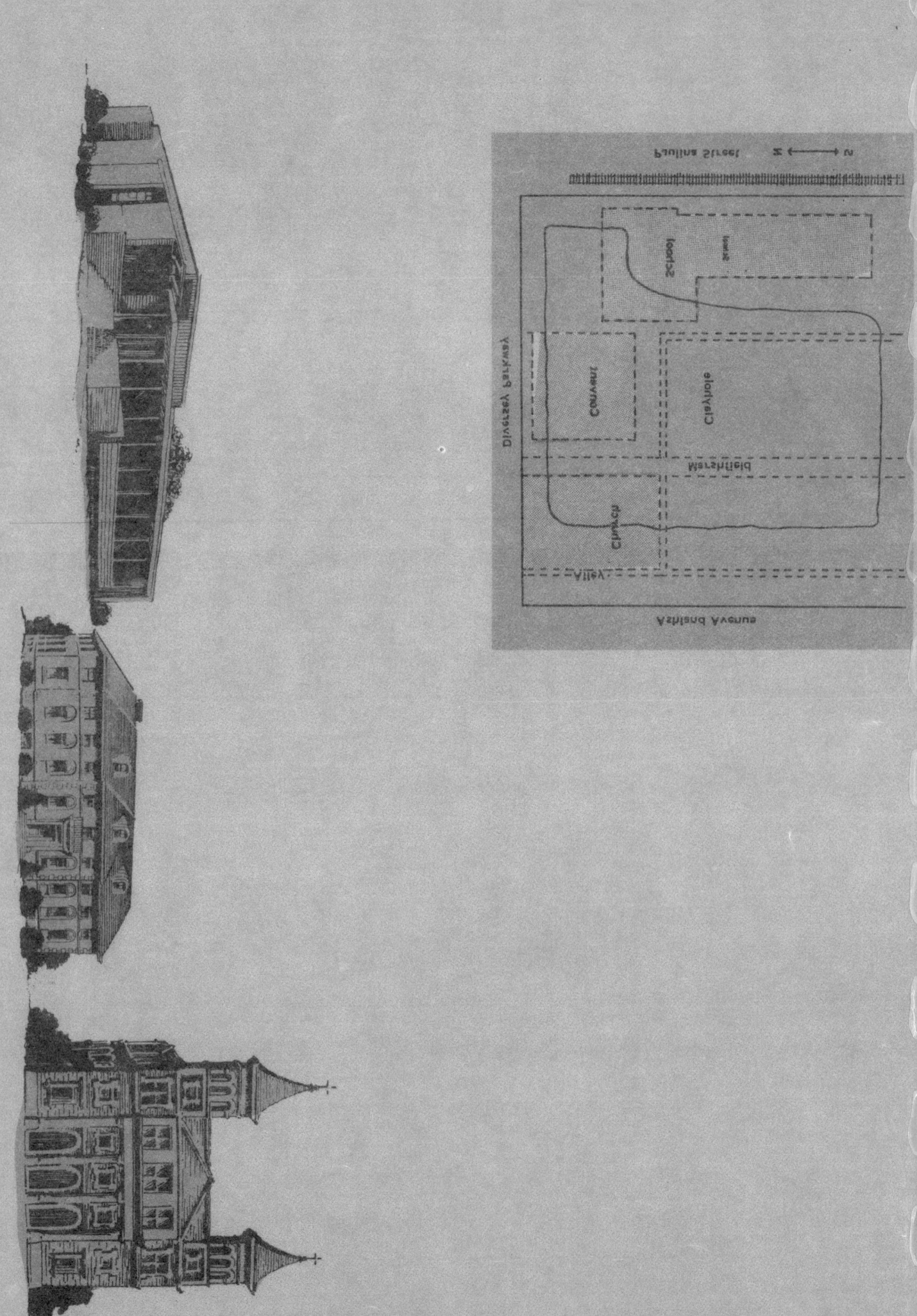

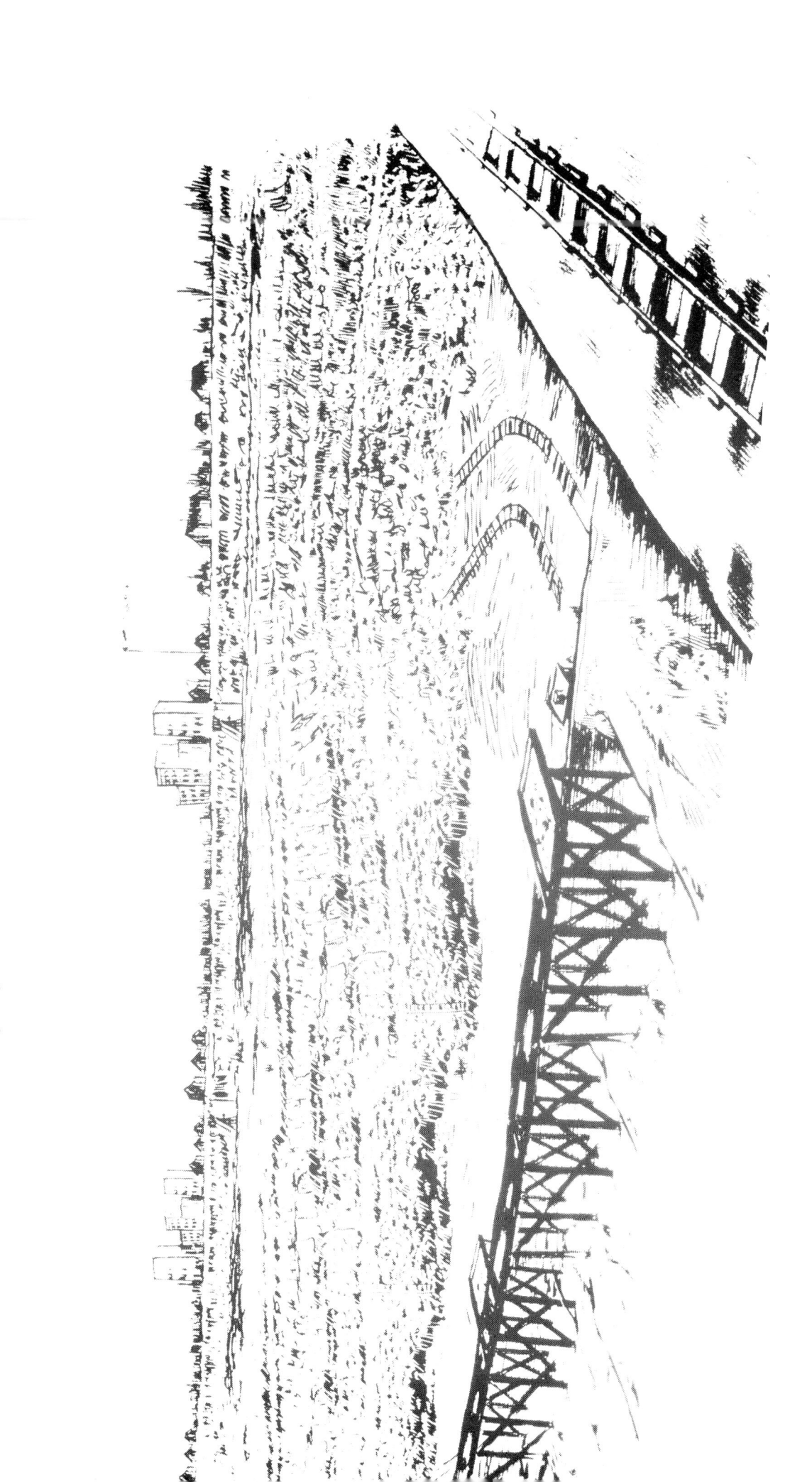

Sketch of a photo taken about 1886 of the future site of St. Bonaventure Convent and School where clay was excavated by the Northwestern Terra Cotta Company.

ST. BONAVENTURE PARISH AREA 1967

In 1927, Father McGuire left St. Bonaventure for All Saints Church and Rev. William P. Long was named to replace Fr. McGuire. Fr. Long was assisted by Rev. Joseph Phelan, newly ordained.

Father Long purchased the property across the street from the church to eventually build a convent for the nuns.

Father Francis Buck, newly ordained, was appointed assistant in June 1934.

In 1935, Fr. Phelan was replaced by Fr. Joseph O'Callaghan and Rev. O'Callaghan was replaced two years later by Rev. Joseph Carton.

The 1930's brought about the closing and destruction of the giant Deering Works of International Harvester Company along the river, and the construction of the Julia Lathrop Homes in its place, the low rise apartment buildings were among the first of their kind to be built in the city by the Chicago Housing Authority; the changing of Robey Street to Damen Avenue, (named after Rev. Arthur Damen, founder of the Jesuit Order in Chicago that eventually became Loyola University); also the construction of the Damen Avenue Bridge across the river to mention only a few.

St. Bonaventure was established; marrying couples, baptizing babies, educating children — all this was done against the background of a rapidly growing, transforming community and a post-war collapse of the economy.

Rev. William Long

Rev. Martin J. McGuire — died March 14, 1928.

May 1927 — Dinner welcoming Father Long.

Top left: November, 1935 wedding of George and Sue Seebacher.
Middle left: January, 1935 wedding of Nick Funck and Ester Seebacher.
Lower Left: 1924 May queen — Louise Duever. Left to right: Corinne Wolf and Mary Reedy Crown bearer: Margaret Smith.
Lower Right: Left to right: Standing: Dan DeZetter, Joseph Gorman and Raymond Stubenrauch. Sitting: Mary Gorman and Viola Stubenrauch. October 26, 1929.

Class of 1922

Class of 1924

Class of 1926

Class of 1925

Class of 1927

Class of 1930

The Second 25 Years

Edward M. Pellicore who graduated from St. Bonaventure's School on June 19, 1925 was the first alumnus ordained for the priesthood — April 18, 1936.

In 1936, the people of St. Bonaventure celebrated the 25th anniversary of the founding of the parish as well as the silver jubilee of Father Long's ordination.

In June 1938, Father Long was appointed pastor of St. Thomas Aquinas Church. But before he left he took responsibility for the financial drive to construct a new convent. His successor was Rev. Vincent J. Moran.

Until 1938, the main floor of the church rested on dirt. An inspection found that the outer walls were sound, but dirt under the inner support had washed away. The parish decided to have six to eight feet of dirt dug out so the walls could be reinforced. Shortly thereafter they decided to dig deeper and create a hall. During those depression days unemployed men from the parish were hired at fifty cents an hour to do the work.

Rev. Vincent J. Moran

Rev. Edward M. Pellicore

1938 — Laida and Albert Marchini.

Top left: Kids in 1939.
Bottom left: Photo taken about 1939 from one of three plays given by the students of St. Bonaventure each year for Christmas, St. Patrick's Day and June Graduation.
Top right: 1938 Majorie Brown married Conrad Theodore on September 14th.

It is significant to note that within a year and a half after he arrived, Fr. Moran had coordinated the effort for the planning and building of the new convent.

1939, Pius XII was elected to the chair of St. Peter. In May the students put on the operetta "Green Cheese," and some of the main characters were: Dell Bedard, Leonard Braband, Joseph Makurat, James Ptack, Helen Duwentester, Mary McHugh, Robert Drew.

Labor forums and schools were held dealing with such subjects as economic doctrines of the church; labor history and problems, just wages, working conditions, retirement benefits and equitable rights for the working man. Many notable professors and experts led the discussions.

Frank Dettloff managed the softball league which held their games at St. Bonaventure Field.

For Thanksgiving the ladies of the Altar and Rosary Society put on the Minstrel Show for the parish.

Originally, the architects planned to place the convent entrance facing the church on Marshfield; because of the clayhole and land fill the building had to be situated on steel and concrete piles to insure it would not sink in later years. It would have to face lengthwise on Diversey where the front half would sit on solid ground.

One afternoon when construction was finally started and the workmen were drilling holes to set the pilings, work was suddenly stopped because the drills were being tangled in springs. The springs, it turned out, were from horse drawn buggies that were discarded years before and used as part of the refuse to fill the clayhole.

The convent was completed in 1939 and dedicated on December 31st.

After the convent was completed, Father Moran purchased the property at Paulina and Diversey from the Northwestern Terra Cotta Works for $25,000.00.

With the acquisition of the property at Paulina and Diversey, Fr. Moran automatically became a member of the Paulina Street Association (formed by the owners of the businesses on Paulina), and was made treasurer — for obvious reasons.

Willie Bargi tells us the lot behind the school today was referred to as "chalk hill"; a large hill developed from waste dumped by the Northwestern Terra Cotta Works; and neighborhood kids would use sleds in the winter and cardboard in the summer as sort of a 30's roller coaster.

With the paving of Paulina, the Italian festivals; cheese throwing contests, Bocce tournaments, dances, etc., which were held in the street, came to an abrupt end.

The 40's started with Samuel Stritch being appointed Archbishop of Chicago.

The school children presented the production "Wonder Puppet" in May, and the cast of characters included: Jack Canty, Therese Fredian, Adolph Ridolfi, Dell Bedard, Bobby Nimietz, James Ptack, Otto Schoenberg, William Leonard, Kenneth Hopp, Leroy Wojciechowski, Edwin Czechorski, Raymond Wiegert and Marilyn Brennecje.

Parishioners took part in a Solemn Holy Hour conducted at Soldier's field where more than 200,000 people attended — praying for world peace.

Each summer camps were operated by the Sisters of St. Joseph at the mother house in LaGrange. The children had the advantages of organized camp life which included horseback riding, swimming, boating, hiking, handicraft all for $10.00 (meals included).

The Young's People Club held many activities during the 40's, such as: picnics, hay rides, dances and beach parties.

1940 Marguerite and Nickolas Rosch.

1940 wedding of Ann Kloss and Harold Borchardt.

Flag Raising ceremony — Altgeld and Marshfield August 30, 1942.

Top left: 1939 St. Bonaventure Convent dedicated December 31st.
Middle left: Left to Right: Sr. M. Bonaventure (Kathleen Hill), Sr. M. Veronica (Caroline Carmody), St. Thomas Agnes (Margaret King), Sr. Anita Jeanne (Mary Frejancz), Sr. Charlotte Marie (Margaret Peggy Smith), Sr. Francis Therese (Lucilla Jankoski) 1942 in LaGrange
Bottom left: Msgr. Eugene F. Lyons.
Bottom right: May 1943 — Beverly Battiste, Sister Roberta, Jeanne Landini

Rubber, paper and steel drives were held as part of the war effort. Food and gas rationing began. At the time, one of our bulletin advertisers sold false teeth for $12.50. Defense plant workers were granted special dispensations from the lenten and Eucharistic fast.

During the World War II the parish was served by Frs. Phillip Cahill, Peter Duffy and Eugene Lyons. Fr. Duffy who had come to serve at St. Bonaventure in 1940 was called to serve as Chaplain in the United States Navy while Frs. Cahill and Lyons both were assigned as professors at Quigley Seminary.

Class of 1939

The Graduating Class of 1931 — the first to graduate in the Church, before that the Hall was always used.

1940 Young People's Club.

WORLD WAR II

During World War II a Military Committee was established, composed of Fr. Moran, John Brown, Bill Jackson, Ed Miller, Joe Paluch with the assistance of Bill Ryan. One of their prime objectives was to compose and publish a monthly paper entitled "News and Views" and send it to every known man and woman from St. Bonaventure serving in the Armed Forces around the world. They also kept and printed an Honor Roll of parishioners and they are as follows:

Honor Roll

Emidio Amidei	Walter Boloe	Walter C. Chekas
C. Anders	Herbert Bonke	William Christiansen
George F. Anderson	Leonard Bonke	Deno Cicci
Gabriel Andreozzi	Harold Borchardt	Mario Cicci
Earl M. Anglemire	*Walter Borowski	Alex B. Ciesinski
Philip "Deedy" Anselmini	Edmund T. Boyk	Harry J. Ciesinski
George Bahr	Joseph Boyk	Hilory Ciesinski
Julius Balash	Lawrence Boyk	Sanders Ciesinski
Theodore R. Balicki	Eugene Boyle	Daniel Cincinelli
William E. Balon	Joseph Boyle	Joseph Ciucci
John E. Bandu	George E. Braeckman	William E. Clark
Mario Bargi	Edward Brankey	Bertram Colbert
Frank Barsi	Norman Brankey	George Cole
Clarence Barts	Raymond Brankey	Emmett Connelly
Gerald Barts	Frank Brocato	Robert Connoly
Lawrence Barts	Bruno Brogi	Lester J. Conoboy
William Barts	*Don J. Brown	Patrick J. Conway
Paul T. Barnum	John Brown	Philip Corbett
Henry Baske	Harold Brown	William Cousins
Max Beavers	Donald Bruno	James Cusack
Iven Bedard	Kenneth W. Burgess	Louis J. Cuzzo
*Henry Beeftink	Leo Burke	Warren Cynova
Ralph Beidron	James E. Butler	Kenneth Dalke
Raymond J. Beitzel	Joseph Campo	Robert Daniel
Alois Belvedere	Henry J. Cauwels	Edward DeCantillon
Raymond Bertolani	Victor L. Capini	Fred A. Deeken
Kenneth Best	Ted Caramelli	Kenneth Delke
Geno Bettini	Richard Cariato	*Joseph Dema
Cynthia R. Biedron	Frank P. Carmody	Vincent DeZetter
Ralph Beidron	John Carroll	William Doherty
Joseph Bieschke	Charles Cauwels	Kenneth C. Dolan
James Boden	Willard Cedar	John Dondalski
Leonard F. Bogacki	Gabriel C. Cemignani	

WORLD WAR II — HONOR ROLL

Andres Douvris
Lawrence Durand
George R. Dwyer
Michael Dwyer
Robert Dwyer
William A. Dwyer
Edward T. Dzike
Kenneth Eddy
Albert Ehmann
Werner Ellman
Herbert O. Evans
Richard C. Faity
Norbert Felski
Deno Fenelli
*Daniel R. Ferguson
Leonard Fester
Michael Filetti
Peter Fini
A. Filetti
Emil Fink
Martin Fiore
Henry Fitzner
James J. Fitzner
Marvin Flugardi
Joseph P. Flynn
James Forde
Edward Formella
John Forssander
Paul Forssander
Joseph Foy
*Martin Foy
Vincent E. Foy
W.S. Foy
Ray Franke
Felix Frateschi
Norman Frederick
Richard Frederick
Eugene J. Fredian
Joseph W. Fredora
Ray Freiboth
Nicholas Funck
Joseph J. Gaba
Walter Gabriel
Frank T. Gagliano
Joseph Gagliano
Louis Gagliano
Edward J. Galuhn
Henry Galuhn
Thomas Gannon

Edward J. Garlin
Anthony C. Gatto
Edward Gdula
Walter Gdula
*Tony Gemignani
John Geni
Leo O. Gentili
Charles Gerhos
Salvador J. Gerovese
Francis H. Gertie
Jacob J. Gertie
Joseph Getz
Joseph Ghimenti
Paul Gilboy
Ralph Gilboy
Clifford Gillis
Winford Gillis
Ernest C. Giltner
Alfred Glauda
Leo Glowienke
William P. Glowienke
James P. Gorman
*John P. Gorman
George Goss
William Goss
John Grady
Walter Groth
George Gryewla
Peter Guerra
John V. Guidotti
Paul Haack
Arthur Habel
James Hannigan
John F. Hannigan
Mary Lillian Hannigan
Richard Hannigan
Michael J. Hansen
Robert A. Hardie
Frederic J. Hart
Thomas Hastings
Norman R. Hayes
George Hebel
Michael Heim
Edward Henry
Arthur Hepp
John J. Herr
George Herr
Richard T. Herrmann
Edward D. Hert

George J. Hert
James D. Hert
John W. Higgins
Edmund B. Hill
John P. Hill
Joseph E. Hill
Kevin Hill
Frank Hollis
William E. Horner
John W. Huck
Irving Huber
Richard Inda
Robert Iven
Tom Jakick
Henry Jakob
Henry C. Jakubiec
Anthony James
Edward S. Jancovic
Clarence Jankoski
Eugene Jankoski
Lawrence Jankoski
Art Jankowski
Joseph Janowitz
Edward Jay, Jr.
Eugene Jennings
James T. Jennings
John Jett
Charles Jungers
*Robert Jurgenson
Bernard Kackert
Nick Kahles
Peter Kahles
Franklin J. Kair
Raymond Kanka
Walter Kapuscinski
George Karl
Frank W. Karl
Walter Karl
Benjamin Kass
Raymond Kawka
Joseph Kazovich
George W. Keil
Jack Keller
William Keller
John Kelly
Martin Kelly
Richard Kelly
Robert H. Kelly
Thomas Kelly

WORLD WAR II — HONOR ROLL

James Kennedy
Maurice J. Kennedy
Bill Kilduff
Tom Kilduff
Coleman M. King
James M. King
Robert J. Klein
J. Klein
William Klein
Joseph P. Kloss, Jr.
Joseph Klost
Ignatius Klostermann
John Klostermann
R. J. Koeneke
John Kolle
John Krerowicz
Richard Krzykowski
Clement Kuerbs
Leroy F. Kulas
Ernest Kunstadt
Paul J. Kuntz
Fred J. Kunz
John Kunz
Tony Kunz
George Kusnicki
Joseph Kusnicki
John A. Lackowski
Louis Ladda
Edward A. Lakowski
Robert Lakowski
Eveo Landini
Renato Landini
Roland Landini
Joseph I. Landini
George J. Lange
Edward L. Langluine
Edwin Laxner
Adam J. Lechman
Joseph Lehman
Edward Lemberg
Aldo Lenzi
George A. Levitzke
John Lewandowski
Andrew Lichter
Jack T. Leitz
Stanley Lindmeier
Herbert R. Litz
John R. Litz
Goerge Livitzki
Paul P. Lubner

William V. Luby
John Lusak
Bill Luthi
John W. Lynch
Norman W. Lynch
Edward Mackey
Fred Magnanenzi
John Magnanenzi
Robert J. Maher
Tom Majewski
Joseph Makurat
Joseph Mancuso
Peter Mancuso
Ralph Manfredi
Anthony Mangiameli
S.A. Mangiameli
Vincent Mangiameli
Sam Mannina
Norbert Marach
Orland Marchini
John Maree
Edward J. Marszalek
Frank P. Marszalek
Joseph Marszalek
Jack Martarano
Victor Matrango
William J. Maxwell
Roy May
Charles I. McCulloch
Bernard McDonough
Emmet McDonough
Eugene McDonough
John J. McDonough
Thomas McDonough
Jerome J. McElboy
John McEvilly
Thomas McEvilly
*John McFarland
John McGuigan
Joseph McGuigan
Joseph McIntyre
Thomas A. McIntyre
Russell McKay
S. Menkol
Frank Mertes
William Meyer
Joe Mignano
Victor Mignano
Florian Milanowski
Robert Milkovich

Charles Minkalis
Richard W. Mischke
Herbert J. Mitzlaff
Joseph A. Morgan
Daniel H. Moscinski
Henry Mount
*Stephen R. Moysis
John J. Mullen
George E. Murphy
Fred Muza
Louis Nadolny
Charles Najjar
Leonard Najjar
John Needham
James Nelson
Geno Neri
Fred Nettnier
Charles G. Netzel
Kenneth Netzel
Charles Neuman
John T. Niebar
Alvin W. Nitsch
John W. Norton
Kenneth Norton
Marion Novelli
Kurt Obee
Daniel O'Connor
James O'Connor
William O'Connor
Thomas V. O'Donnell
William Off
John P. O'Grady
Robert P. O'Ken
Cornelius O'Leary
John N. Olijar
Bernard Olinski
Patrick O'Malley
Robert O'Shanna
Bill Ott
George A. Ott
William Ott
Armando Pagnucci
Alfred Paoli
Attilio Paoli
Ben Paoli
Edward Paolini
Joseph Paolini
Aldo Papucci
Eno Pardini

43

WORLD WAR II — HONOR ROLL

G1192

George N. Paschke	Richard E. Roeder	James Stahl
Arnold Patock	James J. Rogers	Edmund Stempien
Edward Patock	George Rohde	Albert Strmiska
Frank Patock	Dennis W. Roman	Donald Sulzer
Lawrence Patock	Clarence W. Romanowski	Frank Szfranski
Ralph Patock	Eugene Rondoni	Henry Szfranski
*Norbert Patock	Sam Russo	Leroy Szfranski
Clarence J. Pattock	James J. Ryan	Edmund Szmkowski
Edwar Paylor	T.J. Ryan	Edward J. Szmkowski
William Pellus	Willaim D. Ryan	Harry Tarnowski
Herman Penz	Albert Saisi	Donald Taylor
Joseph Peron	Earl H. Salems	Ed Taylor
Ray Perr	Aldo Santoni	George Taylor
George Peskuent	Angelo Santoni	Walter J. Tenner
William Peters	Stephen Sasokovich	Rod Tepich
John Petrinec	Ellard F. Schaefer	Elmer Tessner
Leo Pia	Antone Schell	Anthony J. Theis
Angelo Piagentini	George Schemrowski	Edward T. Tholke
Leo Pionke	Francis F. Schifo	Ellsworth E. Thomson
Angelo Pizzi	Louis Schifo	Peter J. Thompson
Frank Polinski	Nick Schmidt	George Tinucci
Leonard J. Polinski	Tom Schmidt	Matthew Topka
H.P. Pollack	Irvin Schroeder	Francis J. Tossi
John J. Pollack	George Schultz	William J. Touhey
Edward Poppenga	Baldassare J. Scuderi	Charles G. Trocke
Henry Prato	George Seebacher	Michael Tumele
Nestor Prato	Frederick A. Seno	Harry Turco
James Ptack	George Shamroski	William Udrow
George Puccinelli	Dennis J. Shanahan	Leroy Udrow
Thomas S. Radtke	Lawrence Shanahan	Michael J. Uramkin
James J. Ragus	Edward Sikorski	Wilbur F. Uzdrowski
Harold Rambert	Edward Sinkovich	George P. Vernon
Thomas Randazzo	James Sirotzke	Robert Vernon
Harold Raschke	Raymond Skibicki	John Volk
Raymond Reddel	Richard Skibicki	J. Von Buxtaele
Andy Redini	Victor Skibicki	*Anthony A. Walsh
Arthur Rehberger	Albert J. Slakis	Herb Wagner
Arthur W. Reiche	Jack Smith	Joseph Wagner
William J. Reinert	John Smith, Jr.	Peter J. Wagner
John Reiss	J.P. Smullen	Edwin B. Warner
John J. Reitmeier	Charles Snedeker	San Weglarz
John Repp	Mrs. C. Snedeker	Francis W. Weiser
Mathew Repp	LeRoy R. Sobchak	Thomas Wengler
Tom Repp	Robert Soldwisch	Henry M. Wenholz
Martin Resko	Joseph Solin	Daniel Wenserski
Dario Riccomini	Lambert A. Solt	Robert Werner
Adolph Ridolfi	Edward N. Souvigny	George Wiedlin
Thomas A. Riley	*Michael Spadafora	Thomas Wilcox
Walter Roberts	Albert Spinabella	A.J. Wilhelm
Chris Roeder	Rigoletto Spionabella	Edward Willer

44

*George Williams	Eugene S. Wojtezak	Wallace Wright
John Williams	John Wolf	Joseph Wronkiewicz
Charles Witt	William Wolf	Joseph F. Yates
William Witt	John Wolniewicz	Casimir Zabrovitz
G. Wojcieckowski	Thomas Wright	Robert Zentschel

With the unexpected end of the War, "News and Views" abruptly ended. The names that appear in this book were listed in the church bulletin; we regret some names have been omitted because of the cessation of the news letter.

Viola Gorman tells us during the years of the second world war the parish priests would be notified before the family when a young person was killed in action. The priest would then visit the family to break the news.

---

*Of all the men and women who served in the armed forces during World War II from St. Bonaventure, the following were killed in action:

John McFarland technical sergeant. The first graduate of St. Bonaventure School to die of injuries received in battle in 1943.

Anthony Gemignani, private first class. Died during the Italian campaign.

Robert Jurgenson, lieutenant in the Army Air Corps.

Daniel Raphael (Ray) Ferguson, soldier of the Army of the United States. Wounded in action October 9, 1944 and died on October 20th.

Donald Joseph Brown, seaman 2/class United State Navy. Reported missing at Gilbert Island of the Pacific in November 1943. Officially declared dead November 1944.

John P. Gorman, petty officer, United States Navy Reserve died in the Pacific.

Henry Beeftink, sailor in the Navy of the United States died in the Philippines, December 7, 1944.

Joseph Dema, private in the United States Army.

Norbert Patock, Marine private, died on Iwo Jima.

Anthony A. Walsh, Pfc. Killed in the battle on Okinawa.

S. Martin Foy, United States Naval Reserve.

George Williams, sergeant United States Army.

Stephen R. Moysis, Private United States Army.

Michael Spadaforra, private first class, United States Army.

Walter Borowski, sergeant United States Army.

Robert Oshana

POST WAR YEARS

Rev. James Donlan was appointed assistant in May 1945 and Fr. John Kelly replaced Fr. Cahill in November of that year.

The parishioners of St. Bonaventure, along with the citizens of Chicago, celebrated the canonization of Mother Cabrini on September 8, 1946 at Soldier's Field.

The post-war era brought a new surge of growth to the area. The mid to late forties saw the start and expansion of many social and religious organizations: to name a few — The Council of Catholic Women, Inquiry Classes for non-Catholics, Pre-Cana Conferences for Engaged Couples, Altar and Rosary Society, Holy Name Society, Immaculate Conception Sodality, Sacred Heart League, Chi-Rho Club, Young Peoples Club, High School Club and the Aquinas Discussion Club.

Children's activities included Junior Holy Name Society, Children of Mary Sodality and Knights and Handmaids of the Blessed Sacrament.

Fatima Devotions, Sacred Heart Devotions, Forty Hour Devotions and Men, Women and Children's retreats became very popular at this time.

November 1948 brought about the opening of the Parish Library operated and staffed by the ladies of the Altar and Rosary Society. All books and supplies were donated by the parishioners.

Tony Zale spoke at the High School Club in December 1948. Interestingly enough, Mr. Zale trained amateur heavyweight fighter, Willie Bargi, during the war.

1949 saw the advent of the Amateur Hour for parish children sponsored by the Holy Name Society.

At this period in time, the Legion of Decency took very strong stands on what movies were suitable for viewing.

1944 Wedding of Alfred and Josephine Pasquinelli.

1946 Bernice and Raymond Schlapinski.

1946 wedding of Ed and Margaret Galuhn.

1945 Wedding of Edward and Emily Poppenga.

1946 Wedding of Lorraine Pellegrini and Louis Bargi.

Young Ladies Society — 1945.

Marriage of Pearl M. Wilks to Edward Seebacher — February 8, 1947.

May 1948 wedding of Mario and Bernatette Bargi.

Joseph and Pat Palluck — 1948.

May 1948 First Holy Communion of Robert and Roberta Stopa.

June 1946 — (Upper right Left to Right) Rosemary Ward, Gerry Karl, Gerry Groth, Elaine Przyleyski, Audrey Faggi, Sarah McDermott (Front row Left to Right) Helen Lechessi, Pat McClem and Mary Martorano.

Left to Right: Joseph Palluck, Dennis Ryan, Silvio Pellegrini and Fr. Kelly.

In 1949 Mary Motsch was asked to lead a newly formed girl scout troop for a couple of weeks — she stayed on for the next 23 years. Lorretta Roscop led the Junior troop and Lorretta Hilsher the Brownies at that time. There were annual camping trips to Galena and each year the Girl Scouts created a living rosary.

Also in 1949, the Mary and Joseph Circle was started and by the mid 50's as many as 52 members volunteered to help bring handicap individuals to church once a month for Mass and would assist after the Mass at a Mary and Joseph breakfast.

The Boy Scouts, already established, had two troops, Nos. 15 and 64, and were under the very fine direction of Dick Elwart, Al Stoll, Ed Steiner among many others.

1950 brought Fr. Peter Riley to St. Bonaventure.

On November 1, 1950, Pope Pius XII defined and proclaimed the dogma of the Assumption of Our Blessed Lady into the heaven.

With the ever increasing population of the area temporary portable classrooms were set up on the lot behind the Convent.

Parishioners responded generously to appeals for clothing and money to help war victims of Europe and Asia. Over eleven hundred pounds of clothing were collected.

An orphanage was built in Lucca, Italy with the help of contributions from our parishioners.

By the 1950's the school's enrollment peaked to over 1,000 children; there were nineteen nuns living at the convent with the cook.

May 1949 Wedding of Jim and Dorothy Ptack.

Fr. Kelly.

May 1948 Wedding of Lydia and Norbert Kazik with Fr. Kelly.

November 1952 Wedding of Daria and Richard Skibicki.

Easter — St. Bonaventure Choir.

1951 Girl Scout Troop — Mary Motsch standing in middle.

1948 Inaugural of Catholic literature distribution.

May 3, 1947 Corinne Pellegrini and Robert Stasica married.

June 1949 Wedding of Marie and Geno Neri.

January 27, 1951 marriage of Alvin Pellegrini and Tina Koutouzou.

48

Top left — Fr. Moran breaking ground for the school.

Donna M. King and Matthew Ostrowski represented St. Bonaventure on WBBM's "This Way Up" program and Margaret Hilsher was declared 1958 Cook County Spelling Champ.

Albert G. Meyer was installed Archbishop of Chicago on November 8, 1958.

Church records do not exist of parishioners who served in Korea during the 50's. However, Pfc. Michael Conroy, U.S. Army and Pfc. Chester A. Skibicki, U.S. Army were both killed in action.

The cornerstone for the new school was laid April 19, 1953 which was also the same day Fr. Moran celebrated his 25th anniversary as a priest.

As the new school was being planned the clay hole once again played a part in its construction. As with the church and convent, the front of the school, which now sets on the back end of the clay hole, had to be reduced to one story to insure added weight would not sink the school later in years. Where the school is two stories there is solid ground.

Frs. Reading and Sheridan came on board in 1953 and 1954, respectively.

Fr. Sheridan.

Bill Ryan, who attended St. Bonaventure's for eight years, was ordained a priest for the Joliet Diocese in 1955, and said his first mass at St. Bonaventure on June 5, 1955.

Fr. Francis McGrath was assigned to St. Bonaventure in 1957.

In 1959 Rev. Anthony Gaughan replaced Fr. Reading.

In 1957, Fr. Moran was named a Domestic Prelate with the title Right Reverend Monsignor.

St. Bonaventure welcomed the Irish community when its doors were first opened in 1911, and down through the years people of German and Italian descent, among others, added their traditions and customs to the makeup of the church. By the early

Top right — First mass at St. Bonaventure of Rev. William D. Ryan — son of Mr. and Mrs. Dennis Ryan. Concelebrants: Msgr. Vincent Moran (kneeling), Msgr. Lyons, Fr. Ryan and Fr. Joseph Finger.
Middle left — School dedication — Fr. Moran greeting Cardinal Meyer.
Bottom Golden Jubilee of Parish — November 25, 1953 Standing left to right: Srs. Tarcisius Ward, Laetisia Cunningham, Sharon Jackicic, Christopher Jacobs, Marybeth McDermott, Thomas Agnes King, Donna Marie Cannon, Mildred Jackson, Marueen Therese Connaughton, Rosalien Lynak, Jeanine Netzel. Sitting left to right: Srs. Veronica Carmody, Charlotte Marie Smith, Anita Jeanne Ferjancy, Mother Petronilla, Msgr. V.J. Moran, Bonaventure Hill, Frances Therese Jankowski, Immacula Pace.

Fr. Francis McGrath.

1960's the Spanish community was also adding their culture to the ever-changing climate of the church. Fr. Delire recognizing this instituted a Mass to be said in Spanish to accommodate the growing community. And, later in the 1980's Fr. Murray had successfully established a trilingual Mass in English, Italian and Spanish for special occasions. Irregardless of the origins of the people attending mass, St. Bonaventure is Irish — for if you walk into the church on any bright sunny morning, with the sun shining through the windows — the church truly has "the look of the green."

June 1955 — Frs. Donlan, Duffy, Moran and Long.

Fall Festival — 1959

School Dedication

51

Top left: 1957 Jeannette Ptack and Ed Steiner.
Middle left: 1957 wedding of Rose Landini and Chuck Ugel.
Top right: November 1957 wedding of Gloria and Nick Meyer.
Bottom right: 1958 Wedding of Elaine Bernacchi and Jesse Knight.

Top left — Fr. Gaynor.
Top right — Fr. Edwin M. Conway.
Bottom right — 1959 Fall Festival — Eugene McDonough and Kevin Hill with a paying customer.

James G. Gaynor, another young man from the parish, was also ordained a priest.

July 1960, Fr. Edward Conway joined St. Bonaventure replacing Fr. Anthony Gaughan.

The turbulent 60's was brought about principally by the assassination of Malcom X, John F. Kennedy, Martin Luther King, Jr. and Robert F. Kennedy; the long bitter struggle for equality of the blacks; the youth movement; Vietnam and the changes of Vatican II.

Vietnam

Church records do not exist of parishioners serving in Vietnam, however, the following are a few known to have served in the Armed Forces.

Joseph Hill — 1968.

Chester J. Malczewski.

Dennis A. Kirschbaum.

Sean Kilgallan.

50 Years Plus...

In 1961 Msgr. Moran was named pastor of St. Philip Neri Church and Rev. Leo P. Coggins was named to replace him.

Father Coggins was at St. Bonaventure to celebrate the 50th Anniversary of the founding of the church. To celebrate the historical event three Solemn Masses were said: The first in remembrance of the deceased of the parish took place on Friday, November 24, 1962; the second, in appreciation of the living members of the Parish was said Saturday, November 25th; and the third, a Mass of Thanksgiving or Mass of Jubilee was said on Sunday, November 26th.

Bill Barlock and Cecilia Delke headed the committee to put together the Jubilee Ad Book.

Later in 1961 Fr. Lyons left St. Bonaventure parish and Rev. George Helfrich arrived on the scene.

April 8, 1962 was the first drawing of the 50/50 Club. First prize was $75.00; second prize was $25.00; and third prize was $10.00.

Fr. Leo P. Coggins

50th Jubilee Celebration — Left to right: Rev. Leo P. Coggins, Rev. John Kelly, Rev. Francis Buck, Bishop Raymond P. Hilliger, Rev. Eugene Lyons and Msgr. Moran.

1961 Boy and Girl Scout's pancake breakfast.

Fr. George Helfrich.

55

Fr. Lucius B. Delire.

Fr. Colleran.

December 1962 word was received from Alderman Rosenberg of the 44th Ward that a proposed play lot on Paulina Street, south of the school, had passed the City Council and the Park District would begin construction as soon as weather permitted; the play lot was to be blacked topped, fenced and illuminated at night time with basketball, volleyball and tennis courts, swings, slides, etc. for neighborhood children. The proposal failed because the neighbor's petitioned not to have it installed.

Monday, June 3, 1963, the great door of St. Peter's Basilica was closed to signify the death of Pope John XXIII.

Also in June, Fr. Coggins was transferred to St. Raymond de Penafort Church and Rev. Lucius B. Delire was named pastor.

Fr. Delire was ordained a priest on April 7, 1934. He celebrated his first Mass at Holy Name Cathedral — the Mass lasted two-and-a-half hours and has the distinction of being the longest "first" Mass ever said at the Cathedral.

Upon being appointed pastor of St. Bonaventure, he accepted the responsibility of the parish debt which was $163,000.00 principally incurred when the school was built.

July 1963, Fr. McGrath was transferred to St. Francis of Rome Parish in Cicero, Illinois and Fr. James A. Colleran, newly ordained was appointed in his place.

1961 First Girl Scouts to earn the "Marion Award." Patty Maggie, Maryann Ranachowski and Virginia Hemmer.

Graduation breakfast — Rose Dawson.

1961 Wedding of Dorothy and Marvin Miller.

1963 25th wedding anniversary of Laida and Albert Marchini.

1961 25th wedding anniversary of Mr. and Mrs. Steve Hubeck.

1960 "Stars" of St. Bonaventure.

1962 wedding of Fran Kasper and Sal Settipane.

Vatican II

1962-65 — some of the announced aims of the council were to consider reform of the liturgy, religious freedom, ecumenicalism and the place of the church in the modern world. Also, the emphasis on Christian education and the laymans participation in the church resulted in forming St. Bonaventure's first school board in 1969. Elaine Knight described how it began: the first board was made up of school parents and/or parishioners who were nominated and campaigned for each position. They were elected by those enfranchised to cast ballot (the parishioners) in a general election.

The first elected school board follows: Charlotte Mellenthin, Ann Prato, Stan Lindmier, Frank Easpamer, Charles Martinez and Don Waeh.

The main objectives of the school board were to hire a school principal, set tuition rates, raise funds to meet school budgets and establish school policies and procedures.

As a result of Vatican II, Sunday, November 29, 1964 will be remembered for a major change in the Mass — English was used in place of Latin for the first time.

Along with the liturgical changes of the Mass, a new altar was erected facing the people. The sanctuary and missals were also refurbished.

Fr. Conley.

Fr. Eugene Parker.

Fr. Faucher.

1964 Wedding — Adam Sisi, Jeannie and Kenneth Marchini, Ersilia and Paolo Marchini.

1964 Wedding of Emilia and Don Weindorfer.

1964 Football awards: Left to right: Roger Pompa, Roger Hopper, Butch Scholtes, Coach Fr. Collern, Tony Cordaro, Bob Cordaro, Lenny Naumann and Jeff Brociek.

Also as a result of Vatican II, nuns were given more freedom and many of them left community life; therefore, the Sisters of St. Joseph were not able to fully staff the school any longer. Other religious communities were contacted and the school was able to hire two sisters from the Franciscan community. In 1973 of these sisters, Sister Christine Myskow, became principal. However, by 1975 St. Bonaventure was entirely staffed by lay personnel, including the principal, Mr. Robert Davies. St. Bonaventure School was operating with an entire staff of lay personnel including the principal until 1984 when the school board hired Sister Mary Ann Boes who is presently in charge of the school.

February 10, 1965 Father Thomas Conley was appointed to replace Fr. Conway. Fr. Conley was the former editor of the weekly missalette.

The first Spanish Mass began in the chapel in 1966, and to help learn the language, Frs. Parker and Colleran were sent to Mexico.

June 1966, Rev. Eugene Faucher, a full time teacher at Quigley North, replaced Fr. Helfrich as resident. August 23rd saw the arrival of John P. Cody as New Archbishop of Chicago.

The Parish Council was established, chiefly to share with the clergy the responsibilities of the parish and form and coordinate parish policy. The council members helped significantly in the management and functioning of the parish.

The "Hot Dog" mothers: Florence Brociek, Rose Dawson, Mary Paoli, Shirley Finnelli, Gloria Meyer, Norma Ehrenberg, Dolly Galuhn, Pat Bargi, Dolly Bargi and Sophie Lackowski to mention only a few were formed originally to raise money for sports equipment. They met every Wednesday in the school basement and prepared and sold lunch to the children of the school (hot dogs). The original concepts was so successful it continued for years after.

The Chicago Board of Health arranged for polio shots to be administered in the school in February in 1964.

July 5, 1964 Rev. Joseph J. Morin, a former graduate of our school, celebrated his first Mass at St. Bonaventure.

June 20, 1966 Fr. Eugene Parker, newly ordained, came to St. Bonaventure as a regular full time assistant replacing Fr. Eugene Faucher.

January 1967 — Project Renewal was outlined as an Archdiocesan wide fund raising campaign to keep the Archdioceses financially sound. After a successful appeal, pension and insurance plans were established for priests, lay workers and teachers; scholarships were created and area churches could obtain needed revenue in times of crisis.

1972 Council of Catholic Women — left to right — Norma Ehrenberg, Barbara Hoehne, Bernice Schlapinski and Irene Szymczak.

1969 Wedding of John and Anita Wurbia.

Fr. Joseph B. Morin.

1968 Wedding of Steve and Trudy Hubeck.

John Kelly was voted unanimously for the 1967 Senior Citizen Hall of Fame by the Lake View Citizens Council. Mr. Kelly was a very active parishioner here at St. Bonaventure working in the Holy Name Society and Mary and Joseph Circle.

In 1969 Rev. James Colleran was transferred to special Spanish work and Rev. John P. Cunningham was assigned as resident with special work in the National Clergy Council on Alcoholism with a permanent office of the N.C.C.A. in the old school.

Rev. Robert Baranowski, a graduate of our school was ordained in Rome on December 19, 1969 and said his First Mass at St. Bonaventure July 5, 1970.

January 1970, with the economy declining and the country heading into a recession, Fr. Delire, together with pastors of various other neighborhood churches and local community leaders, established the Diversey Emergency Pantry. The pantry, located in the Lathrop Homes, provided bags of non-perishable food on an emergency basis to people of the community. The pantry, still in existence today, was far ahead of its time. It was the first pantry on the north side and has served as a model for other pantries since. Assisting Fr. Delire in establishing the pantry from St. Bonaventure were: Al Priami, Paul Kirschbaum, Marie Kirschbaum, Danny Fitzmaurce, Marie Carlise, Al Adams and Minnie Johnson.

1970 brought a new assistant pastor, Fr. Lawrence Malcolm, who helped establish a branch of the Italian Catholic Federation for families of Italian descent at St. Bonaventure. Fr. Malcolm was also responsible for implementing the "dunk tank" at the carnivals and encouraged all parishioners to vent their frustrations when he was one of the featured V.I.P.'s.

Rev. Robert Baranowski

July, 1968 wedding of Rita Kirschbaum and Nick Guttilla with Paul and Marie Kirschbaum, Mary and Peter Guttilla.

Rev. John P. Cunningham

Rev. Lawrence Malcolm

Top left: Rev. Herbert J. Boesen
Top middle: James McDermott
Middle left: 1974 wedding of Kathy Karl and Nick Roeder
Top right: Fr. Malcolm with Steve Oleszizuk

The school year in 1971 started with St. Bonaventure School being selected as one of fifteen Catholic schools in the Chicago area to present the Individually Guided Education (IGE) program to replace the old graded system.

Under the direction of Sister Diann Musial the program of education was designed to meet the individual needs of each child rather than as first, second or third graders. Children worked in smaller groups and parents became more involved. The program proved to be too extreme and was later dropped.

While interior of the church was being cleaned and redecorated in 1972, the convent was vacated by the Sisters of St. Joseph and, with the old rectory gradually deteriorating, the priests and rectory office staff moved into the convent building which then became the rectory. The Old rectory building was rented out in 1973 to the Holy Cross Fathers and was renamed "The Moreau House." In 1983 the Moreau House was torn down and the property rented by Frank DeBartolo of Ash Manor Restaurant for a parking lot.

A new dimension was added in 1972 in the form of a Square Dance Club.

Rev. Eugene Parker was transferred to St. Aloysius Parish in 1973, Fr. Stephen was assigned to take his place and Rev. Herbert Boesen, retired pastor of St. Joseph and Ann Parish, came to assist in his retirement.

In 1974, the school debt was repaid, the 700th anniversary of the death of Saint Bonaventure was celebrated — in one-hundred degree heat — on Sunday, July 14th, with Archbishop, John Cardinal Cody Celebrating the Jubilee Mass. Fr. Delire celebrated his 40th Anniversary of Ordination, and through the efforts of Bill McDermott, custodian, and Ed Steiner, Gary Glowlenke, John Santos, Dom Cantore, Ruben Gomez, Tom Bickel, Tom Bargi, Jim Fannuci, Nick Ehrenberg, Tony and Bill Coughlin, Gary Prato, Ted and Mark Paoli, John Tramutola, Frank Dawson and Ken Schlapinski — the "Parish and School Maintenance Committee" the old gym was renovated and turned into a modern athletic facility.

We all learned a lesson in the art of running a Rummage Sale from Fr. Malcolm, Florence Brociek, Betty McMeekin and Norma Ehrenberg in 1974 when fund raising reached new heights.

Bingo, also a tradition handed down through the years, originally was run in the hall under the church and was first organized by Wally Witt. The pews and kneelers were temporary in order to be moved on bingo days until the school was built and bingo transferred to the school hall. There were years, however, when bingo was renamed the Match Game because Bingo was declared illegal.

Top left: September 1974 wedding of Rick and Kathy Bargi.
Middle left: 1973 — 50th wedding anniversary of Frank and Johanna Daniel.
Bottom left: 1977 "Funny" Fashion Show.

June 1976, Fr. Malcolm was transferred to St. Theresa Parish in Palatine, Ill. Fr. Thomas A. Moran was appointed to replace him.

The Legion of Mary began in the chapel in 1976.

The Sharing Program was instituted in 1977 whereby parishes located within the Archdiocese who were financially secure would adopt parishes that were not. St. Bonaventure was adopted by St. Theresa of Palatine and in turn helps St. Ambrose Parish. The program extended beyond financial aid to other areas such as sharing liturgies; CCD instruction; social, cultural and athletic activities.

Rev. Charles Fanelli moved to St. Bonaventure in February of 1978 in order to be closer to the Archdiocesan Pro-Life Office in downtown Chicago. Even though his energies were directed at the church's effort to save the unborn here in Chicago, he helped St. Bonaventure in many ways; he reorganized the Liturgy Committee, was a driving force at Bingo, was very active in the Italian Catholic Federation and instructed the Lectors and Commentators. It was through his efforts the statue of Saint Gemma Galgani came to St. Bonaventure. He stayed at St. Bonaventure for seven years and then was appointed pastor of St. John Vianney Church.

Middle left: Rev. Thomas A. Moran
Top middle: Rev. Charles Fanelli.
Middle right: May 1976 wedding of Sue and Tom Pekara.
Bottom right: 1976 Dedicating traffic light at Diversey and Paulina. Right to left: Candy Peterson, Ernie Peterson, John Peterson, Bernie Hanson, George Puccinelli, Terry Gabinski, (Alderman), Angelo LaPaglia, Fr. Delire and Ted Kozio, Ward Superintendent.

1978 the world mourned the loss of Pope Paul VI, Giovani Battista Cardinal Montini. After election to the papacy on June 21, 1963, he inherited a church caught up in sweeping revolution. When he died, his legacy was a church that had seen great change but had reaffirmed its center.

The College of Cardinals met in 1978 and elected Albino Cardinal Luciani Pope John Paul I on August 6th. Unfortunately, he lived only 33 days into his papacy and died suddenly.

Monday, October 16, 1978, Cardinal Carol Wojtyla was elected 264th Pope of the Roman Catholic Church. At 58, he was one of the youngest men to be elected pontiff in modern times and the first non-Italian since 1522. Taking the name of John-Paul II, he was the first Pope from Eastern Europe and the first from Poland. A man for all seasons, all situations, all faiths, a modest superstar of the church, he toured the United States for seven days in the fall of 1979 visiting Chicago for 38 hours and topping off his visit with a Mass in Grant Park for a crowd of approximately 500,000.

On July 1, 1978 Father Delire was named pastor emeritus and Rev. Michael J. Murray was appointed pastor.

Fr. Murray was ordained in 1955. His early work involved him with the American Indians and Appalachian transplanted families in the Uptown and near northwest side of Chicago.

Later, Fr. Murray was the founding editor of the monthly missalette which is now used in eighty-five

Top left: 1977 wedding of Peggy Stubenrauch and Chet Kulis.
Middle left: Rev. Michael J. Murray
Bottom left: Welcoming Rev. Murray with Rose Foster.

1978 Wedding of Linda and Robert Cummings with Ed and Margaret Galuhn

Fiftieth Wedding Anniversary of Joseph and Viola Gorman — October 14, 1979.

Rev. Michael J. Boehm

percent of the parishes in the United States today.

He was Chaplain of the Young Christian Workers, a professional marriage counselor, worked as a neighborhood director of the Catholic Youth Organization and was a Papal Volunteer Organizer.

Given the choice of more involvement with specialized work or being a full-time parish priest the choice was always for parish work.

While at St. Bonaventure, Fr. Murray has been responsible for the new organ and exterior bells, but more importantly he has put into practice some innovations that have stabilized the school and church and made them more sturdy and resilient in this ever-changing community and parish.

Wedding of Karen Bargi and Ernie Papucci.

1981 Wedding of Ursula and Garry Chelette.

1983 Wedding — Left to right: Ivan Del Rio, Myrian Del Rio, Felicita Roman, Tito Roman and Fr. Boehm.

25th Wedding Anniversary of Felicita and Tito Roman with Fr. Boehm.

50th Anniversary celebration of Nick and Ann Mei.

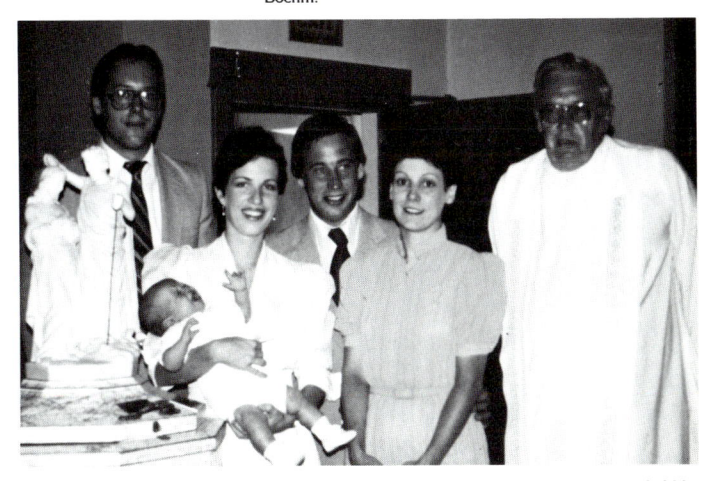

1981 Baptism — Bob and Margie (Ehrenberg) Gernhofer, Rick and Niki (Leiding) Gernhofer with Fr. Murray.

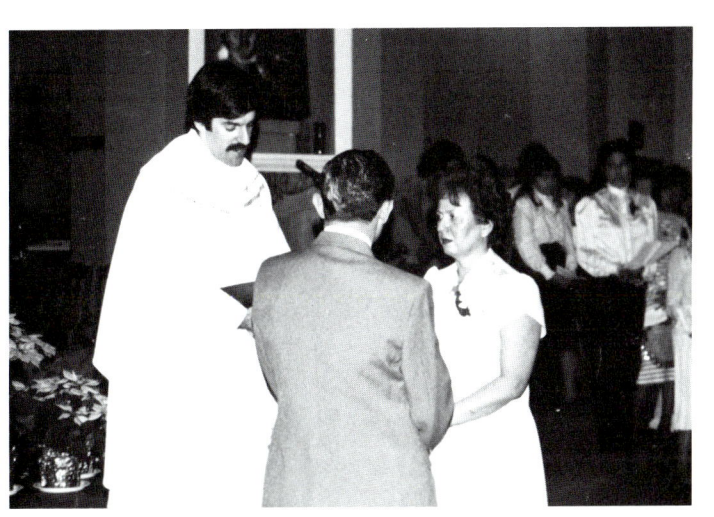

25th Wedding Anniversary of Jose and Lydia Cintron with Fr. Boehm in 1983.

Fr. Michael J. Boehm joined St. Bonaventure Parish in October of 1980 as an associate pastor. He was ordained in 1975 and was transferred from St. Mary of the Lake parish.

April 25, 1982 John Patrick Cardinal Cody died of cardiac arrest. After his arrival as archbishop of Chicago in 1965, he was elevated to the College of Cardinals in June of 1967 thus becoming Chicago's fourth cardinal. He celebrated his fiftieth anniversary as a priest on December 8, 1981.

In July Chicago welcomed Archbishop Joseph L. Bernardin of Cincinnati to fill the post left open by the death of John Cardinal Cody, and on February 2, 1963 he was elevated to Cardinal.

Father Delire celebrated his 50th anniversary as a priest on April 7, 1984.

Father Richard T. Simon came to St. Bonaventure as an associate pastor in 1984.

Born in LaGange, Illinois, he attended St. Xavier School before studying for the priesthood at the archdiocesan seminaries. He was ordained in 1975. Aside from teaching, he was also involved in the charismatic movement for several years.

The newest addition to the St. Bonaventure family is Saint Gemma Galgani; a statue of her likeness is presently located in the back of church furnished by Lina Bianchi in memory of her son, Frank Bianchi.

October 1983 Wedding of Martha and Dennis Neri.

1984 Fr. Simon and Christina Cruz.

1983 Wedding of Jose and Tina Cintron with Fr. Boehm.

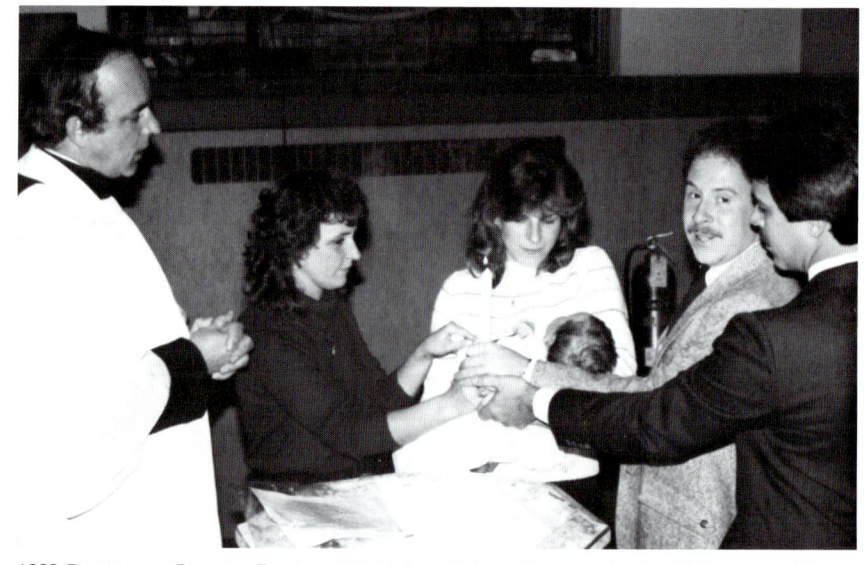

1983 Baptism — Parents: Frank and Patricia DiMatteo; Godparents: Daniel Bargi and Sharon Ruta.

Paul Battiste — 1983.

1984 Baptism of Nicole Marie Cintron

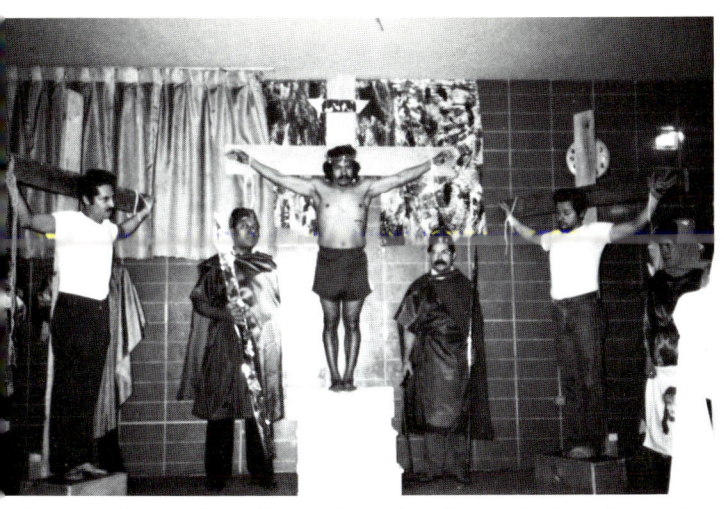

St. Gemma was born March 12, 1878 in Tuscan near Lucca, Italy, she was the fourth of eight children. Her girlhood was marked by various severe physical illnesses and the loss of both parents. Her faith in God increased with each setback. On the eve of the Feast of the Sacred Heart in 1899 Gemma received the marks of Our Lord's five wounds which caused her intense suffering. She died on Holy Saturday, 1903, at the age of 25. She was canonized by the Pope Pius XII on the Feast of the Ascension 1940.

1985 Easter Passion: Pedro Olea — Jesus Jose Crespo, Santiago Correa, Jose Alvares and Antero Santos.

1984 50th Wedding Anniversary of Steve and Bernice Bush shown here with their great-granddaughter Katherine Ahern and her "kid."

1985 Marguerite and Nick Rosch 45th Wedding Anniversary.

30 Years Later — June 1985 celebrating his anniversary Rev. Bill Ryan is photographed with his 6th grade teacher, Sr. Liguori.

1985 Cathy and Tom Pattullo.

Lina Bianchi, Saint Gemma and Eleanor Ori.

Frank Bianchi in whose memory the statue of Saint Gemma is donated.

1985 Celebrating the Feast of Our Lady of Guadalupe (Patroness of Mexico). Amado Barajas and Manuell Cijneros.

Wedding September 1986 Left to Right: Tito Roman, Felicita Roman, Fr. Simon, Tony Adamowski, Efran Feliciano and Iraida Feliciano.

Carnival parade.

Jerry Lapinski, Mary Motsch and Wanda Weigel.

Carnival Guests — Bob Kilcullen and Mike Ditka with Dorothy Ptack in 1963.

Carnival Guest — Johnny Morris with Dorothy Ptack in 1963

Carnival Time

St. Bonaventure's annual carnivals have become a tradition on the Northside. The first carnival started as early as 1930 with Father Long and carnivals have continued down through the years except in 1960 and 1961 when Cardinal Meyer banned gambling which included the jar games. In the early days, the games and rides were set up on the ground presently occupied by the convent. Carnival preparation would start early in January with dedicated carnival committees planning special events, promotional gimmicks and advertising announcements. Genevieve Hill recalls the carnival workers (parishioners) after working all day at regular jobs would carry out the prize merchandise and stock the booths every night, then take everything back to the school at the end of the evening. They also had to be on guard for sudden storms to protect the merchandise from the elements. In the late 50's, Fr. McGrath and Beverly Battiste were instrumental in establishing St. Bonaventure's Carnival as the largest on the Northside which was one of the key factors in bringing about a new era of prosperity to the church and school.

In 1967 a new Carnival Committee was formed. Twenty years later, three members of this Committee — Richard Elwart, Dorothy Gatoo and Patricia Foley — remain active; a fourth, George Seebacher was active until his death in January 1983. These people, together with many others who joined the Committee for a few years at a time, planned and operated successful carnivals, fall festivals, Las Vegas Nights and the first "Taste of" at St. Bonaventure. They have enjoyed the co-operation of the parishioners and friends of St. Bonaventure Parish for without this spirit, no fund raising activity could be a success.

After the convent was built, the carnival site shifted to the corner of Diversey and Paulina. The convent basement was used as carnival headquarters before the school was built.

Father Moran would rent big flood lights to attract people driving through the area, and Father Delire would insist on having the very tallest ride so it could be seen from the Kennedy Expressway.

AROK the famous robot from Palos Hills, was a guest at the 1977 carnival. Arok was the answer to a housewife's prayer. He could vacuum the floors, take out the garbage and do numerous other tasks around the house. After watching a demonstration of his activities, the patrons at the carnival had a chance for a close-up look at Arok.

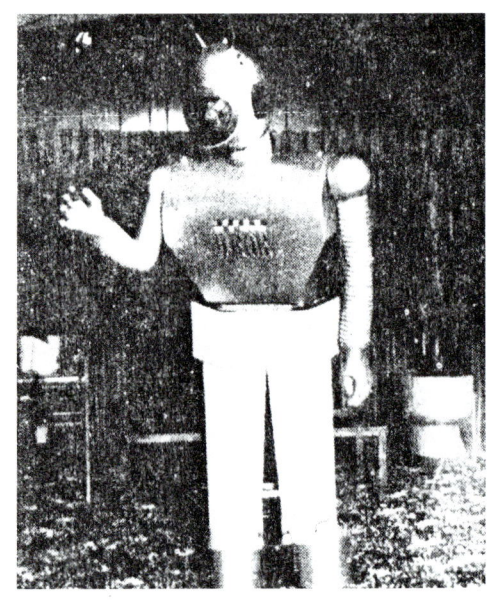

Arok — the featured guest at the 1977 carnival.

Two Chicago Cubs baseball players, Larry Bittner and Mickey Kelleher, made a guest appearance at the 1980 carnival.

CARNIVAL WORKERS

BINGO WORKERS

50/50 Club

50/50 Club — Pictured top left: Val Papucci; top right: Leo Ranachowski; bottom left: Darlene Dorsch; Middle: Dick Elwart; bottom right: Mary Motsch.

| HARRY PRATO | ALBERT MARCHINI | PAUL KIRSCHBAUM | CARL WIRTZ | LAWRENCE BARTS | BERNARD KACKERT |

| ALBERT PRIAMI | STANLEY LINDMEIER | DOUGLAS BASCHIERE | THOMAS MALONEY | ARTHUR HITTERMAN | JOHN FINLEY |

| LEO RANACHOWSKI | FRANK DAWSON | CHARLES POLTROCK | FRANK TOBIN | RICHARD ELWART |

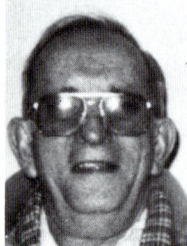

USHERS

Our Jubilee Year — 1986

Fall of 1985 started with planning, committee organizations, etc.

Chicago residents forgot how bad January weather could be when the Chicago Bears ended the football season at the Superdome in New Orleans winning Superbowl XX — a first in Bear history. Also in January, the nation mourned the loss of Challenger space shuttle and seven astronauts, the Titanic was found 13,000 feet below the surface of the North Atlantic.

In early spring, Halley's comet made its return from around the sun swinging by the earth before heading out in space — the last time the comet appeared St. Bonaventure Church was being constructed. The long awaited repaving of Diversey Parkway was finally started just in time to close the street for our carnival.

After months of restoration, the Statue of Liberty and Ellis Island were re-dedicated on July 4th by President Ronald Reagan celebrating the 100th birthday of Liberty. St. Bonaventure couldn't physically be

1986 Rev. Donald Nevins — Spanish Ministry and Liturgy.

Carnival Committee 1986 — Front row — left to right: Dorothy Gatto, Pat Foley and Rose Foster. 2nd row: Ralph Foley, Tom Tappings, Art Hitterman, Dick Elwart and Patrick Kelly.

Church Choir of 1986: Kathy Stubenrauch, Barbara Giannoni, Josephine Pellegrini, Isabel Collazo, Mary Scuderi; 2nd row: Richard Elward, Corrine Stasica, LuAnn Kowar, Joan Brown, Ed O'Connor; 3rd row: Andy Pecson, Richard Kunz, Thomas Bickel, Tony Georgeson.

Spanish Choir — Tony Castro, Aidy Berrios, Maneul Berrios, Nery Castro, Haidee Aguirre, Nelly Dejesus, Rogelio Castro, Inelisse Aguirre.

A resolution

adopted by **The City Council** of the **City of Chicago, Illinois**

Presented by ___ALDERMAN TERRY GABINSKI___ on ___NOVEMBER 13, 1986___

Whereas, St. Bonaventure Parish, one of the most spiritually influential and active religious institutions on Chicago's great Northwest Side, was established 75 years ago; and

WHEREAS, Located at 1641 W. Diversey Avenue, St. Bonaventure Church has throughout most of this century earned the respect, confidence and gratitude of the neighborhood which it has so diligently served; and

WHEREAS, Currently headed by the Rev. Michael Murray, Pastor, St. Bonaventure Parish remains a continuing source of inspiration to its parishioners and to the neighborhood which benefits so considerably from its presence; now, therefore,

Be It Resolved, That we, the Mayor and members of the City Council of the City of Chicago, gathered here this 13th Day of November, 1986, A.D., do hereby congratulate St. Bonaventure on the occasion of the Parish's 75th Anniversary, and extend to this great Parish our very best wishes for many more years of fulfillment and success; and

Be It Further Resolved, That a suitable copy of this resolution be presented to St. Bonaventure Parish.

_____
MAYOR

_____
CITY CLERK

Commentators and Lectors — 1986 Sitting left to right: Andy Pecson, George Kasper, Roy Metclaf and Fr. Murray. Standing left to right: Ed Steiner, Frank Dawson, Tony Georgeson, Bernice Schlapinski, Frances Begnuche, Kathy Stubenrauch, Ray Stopa, Irene Priami, Jeanette Kulanda, Doug Baschiere, Ann Baschiere, Frank Renkert and Ron Maziarika.

Photo to right: Officers of Council of Catholic Women — Left to right: Norma Ehrenberg, Tecla Monahan, Bernice Schlapinski, Beverly Battiste, and Jerry Peterson.

Photos left: Italian Catholic Federation: Sitting Left to right: Licena Matteucci, Josephine Bienias, Mara Pacini, Nella Parenti, Josephine Fanucchi, Dolores Kubat, Gladys Scharneck, Laura Maninfior, Rose Ridolfi; 2nd row: Elisa Gerignani, Egitina Bartolomei, Laeda Marchini, Nelda Biagi, Mary Bargi, Rina Marcheschi, Lina Bertoncini, Lea Paoli, Esmeralda Lamberti, Mary Galli. Not pictured: Anna Battiste, Beverly Battiste, Emilia Boni, Ann Calabrese, Amelia Chiappa, Giorgia Cortopassi, Katie Cunningham, James Fanucchi, Nancy Flosi, Margaret Galuhn, Premetta Ghilardi, Gina Giannotti, Pietro Giannotti, Eleanor Kowalski, Giuseppe Landini, Adele Lindmeier, Lola Marchetti, Anna Mei, Settima Papucci, Louise Paveglio, Mariza Pierazzi, Imola Pierucci, Olga Ratti, Fr. Simon, Jeanne Wehrheim.

present but we were officially entered into the Register of Contributors for the restoration in the statue's archives.

As summer was drawing to an end activities celebrating the diamond Jubilee year started to intensify with a trip to Holy Hill, a parish picnic, a potluck dinner, a wedding anniversary day for all people married at St. Bonaventure, a memorial mass for deceased relatives and friends and a reunion day for all St. Bonaventure alumni.

October began with Terry Gabinski, alderman, introducing a Resolution in the Chicago City Council commemorating St. Bonaventure's 75th Jubilee.

The culmination of a year of planning started on Saturday, October 11th with an enormous parish dinner dance at the Venice Halls and followed Sunday with Mass celebrated by Archbishop Timothy Lyons and a reception in the school hall.

Luncheon Committee for the 1986 Fashion Show presented by the Council of Catholic Women.

Legion of Mary — Elpedio Maldonado, Bernadina Maldonado, Manuel Berrios, Maxinino Lebron, Bernarda Lebron, Tito Roman, Felicita Roman, Lorenzo Rodriguez and Ester Rodriguez.

Sacristy Committee — Left to right: Josephine Osceike, Elda Gugliotta and Wanda Miller.

Rev. Edmon Siedlecki — Sacristy.

Scoutmasters: James Barrientos, Mike Dooley, (Officer Friendly — 19th Police District) Daniel Seng, Jose Alvarez.

School Faculty — Seated left to right: Ken Stanhibel, Joan Hogan, Sr. Mary Ann Boes, Peggy Fahey, Lois Graham-McHugh, Joan Valdez. Standing: Colleen Kennedy, Eileen O'Brien, Rosemary Rimar, Maridan Gilmore, Francine Johnson.

Photo to right: 75th Anniversary Committee: 1st row: left to right: Elvira Santiago, Viola Gorman, Laede Marchini, Juan Efrain Feliciano, Felicita Roman, Luey Perez, Andy Pecson, Josephine Osiecki, Wanda Miller, Elda Gugliotta; 2nd row: Doloris Kirschbaum, Rose Foster, Irene Priami, Marie Kirschbaum, Fr. Delire, Fr. Murray, Ivelise Aguirre, Pat Bargi, Iraida Feliciano, Lydia Cintron, Nery Castro; 3rd row: Tecla Monahan, Frank Dawson, Kathy Stubenrauch, Ray Stopa, Haydee Aguirre, Manuel Berrios, Rogelio Castro, Tito Roman, Bernardina Maldonado, Elpidio Maldonado. Not pictured: Bernice Schlapinski, Gerry Peterson, Norma Ehrenberg, Gloria Meyer, Fr. Simon, Andero Santos, Roy Metclaf, Angelo Pierucci, Beverly Battiste and Al Krauser, the photographer, who was taking the picture.

Prayer Group — Sitting left to right: Nelly Castro, Felicita Roman, Ester Rodriguez and Carmen Mendez. Standing left to right: Manuel Berrios, Ragelio Castro, Tito Roman, Aida Berrios, Iraida Felician, Fr. Simon, Angel Mendez, Efrain Feliciano and Lorenzo Rodriquez.

THE JUBILEE MASS

81

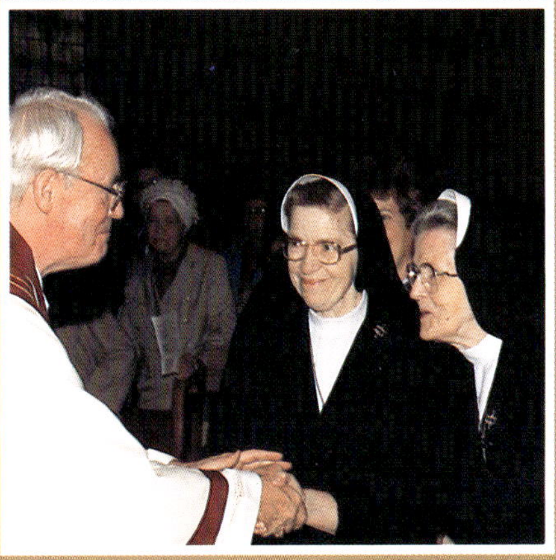

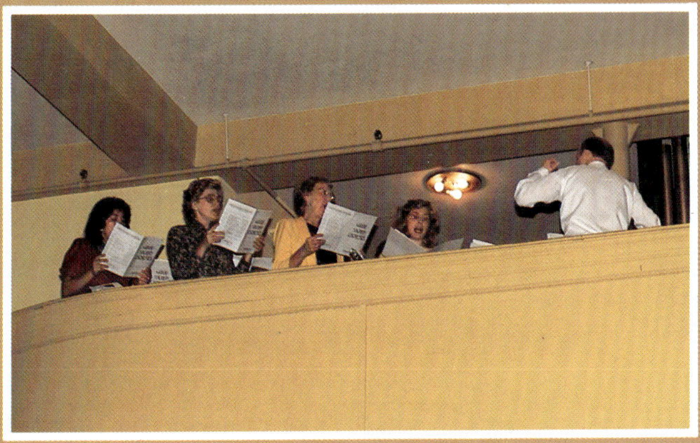

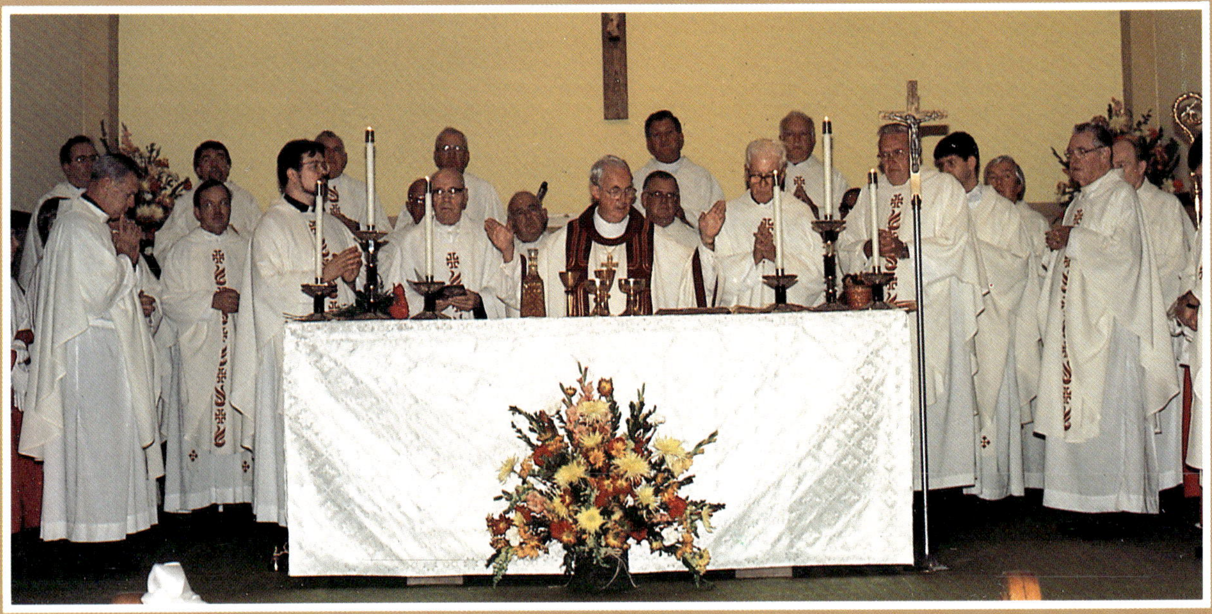

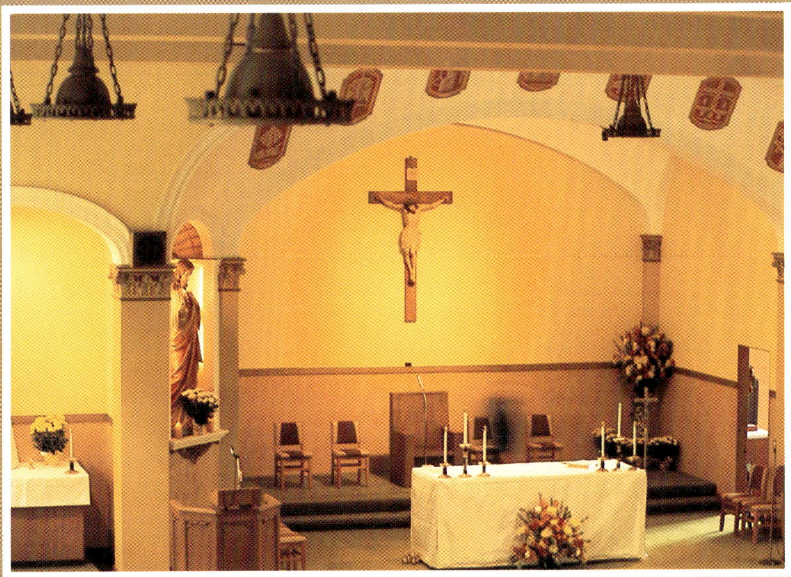

Jubilee Dinner and Dance

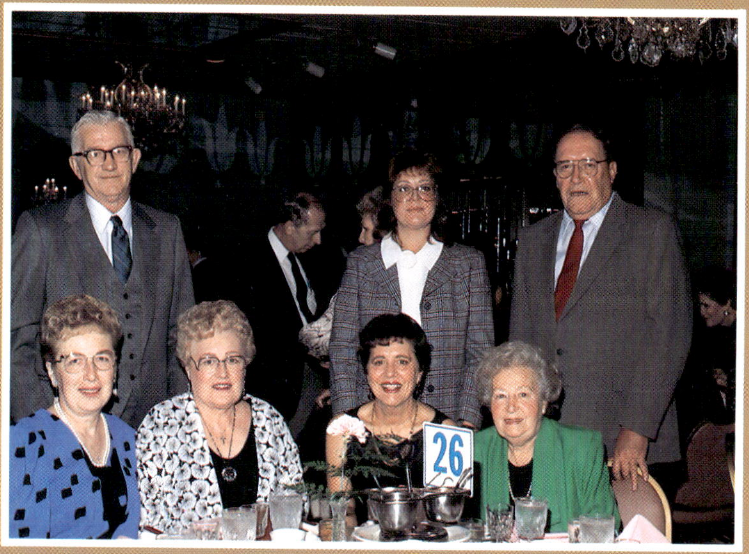
26

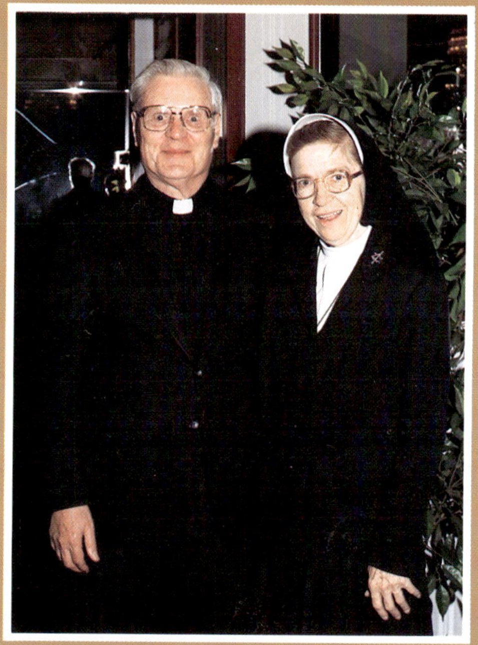

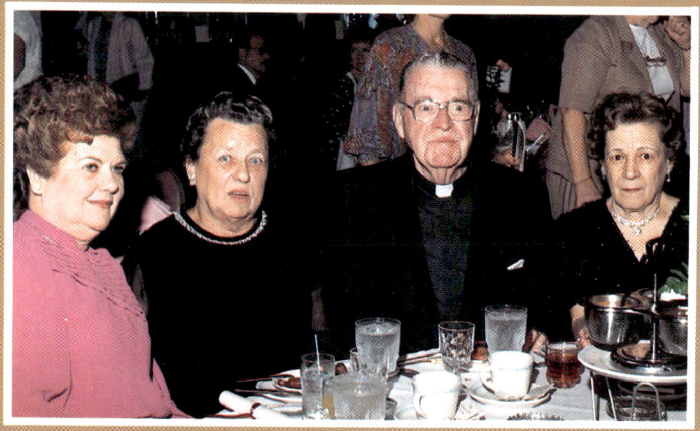

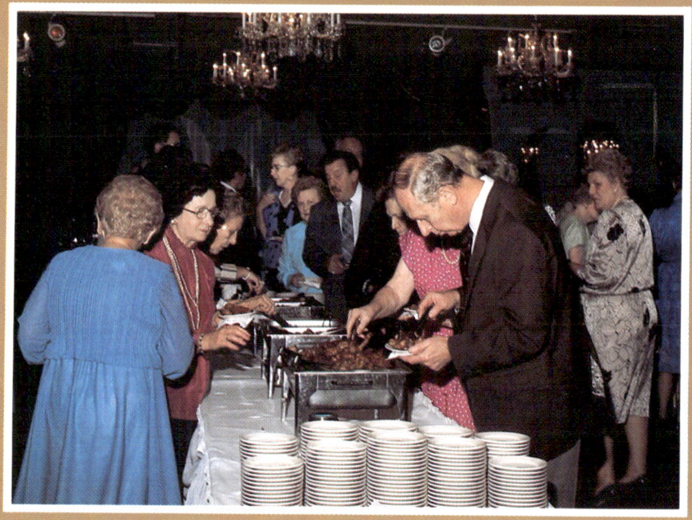

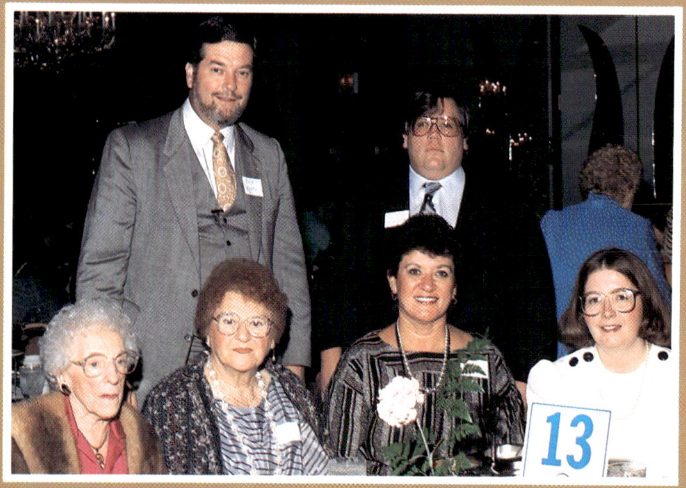
13

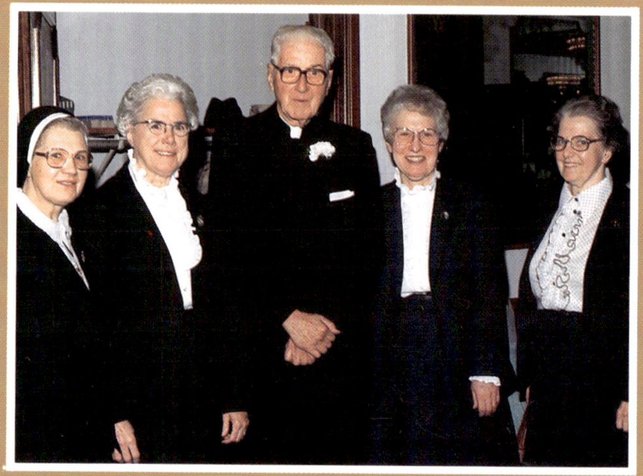

85

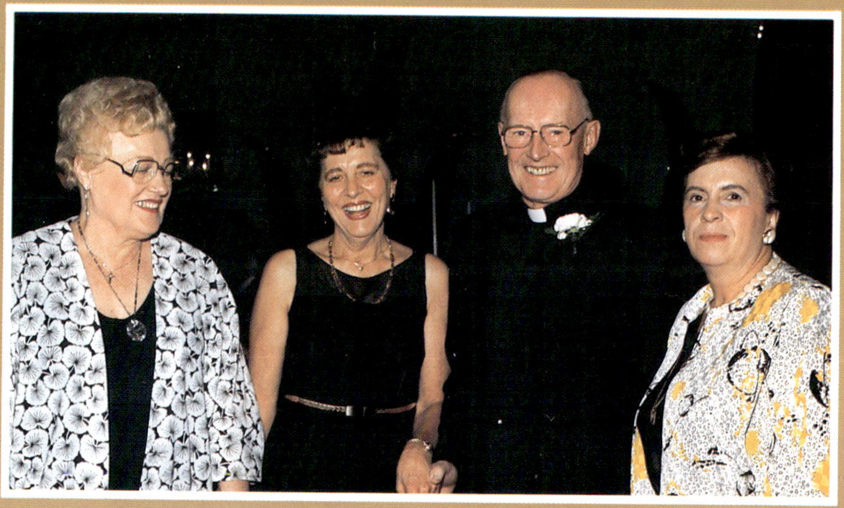
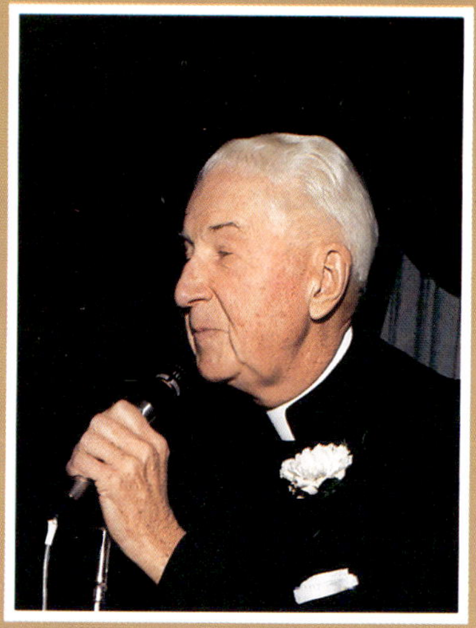
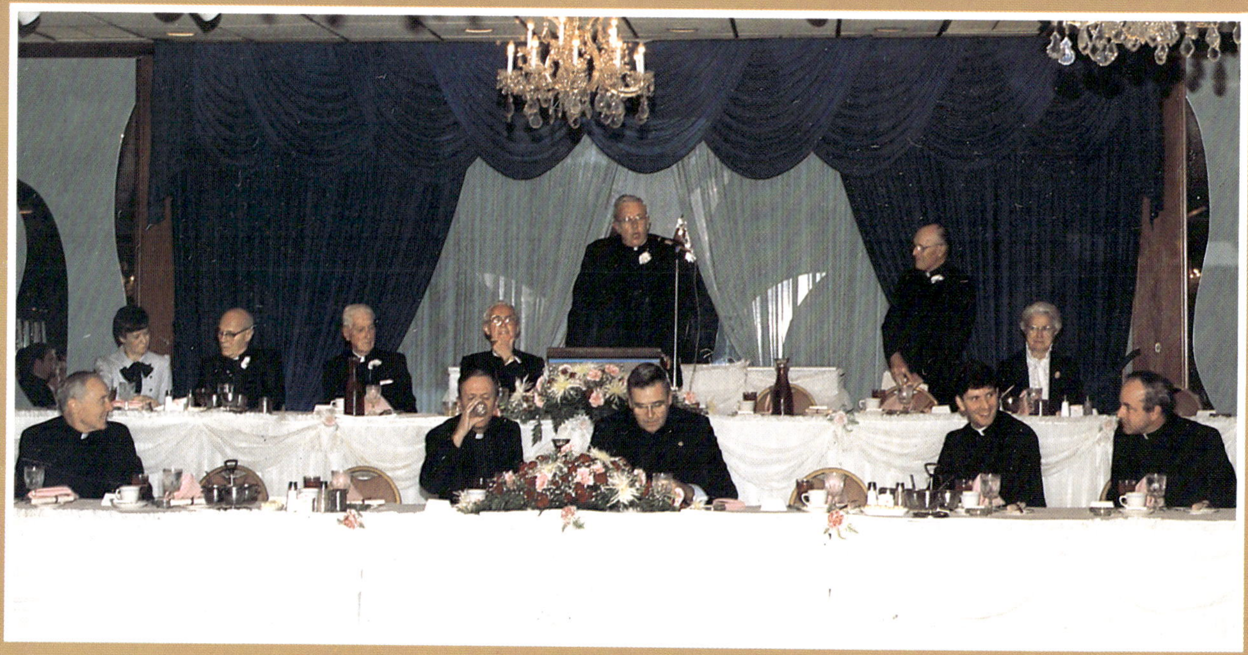
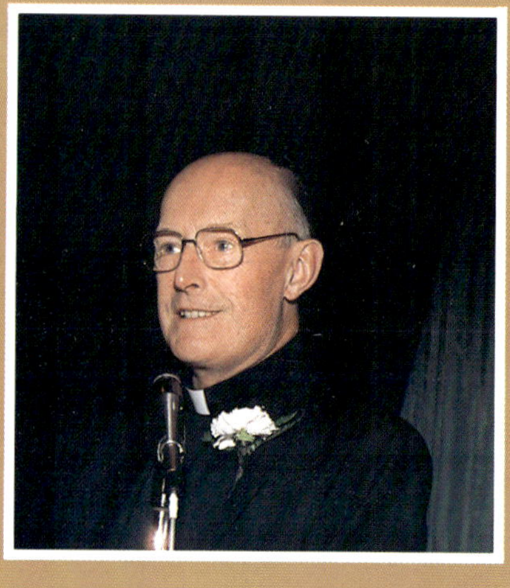
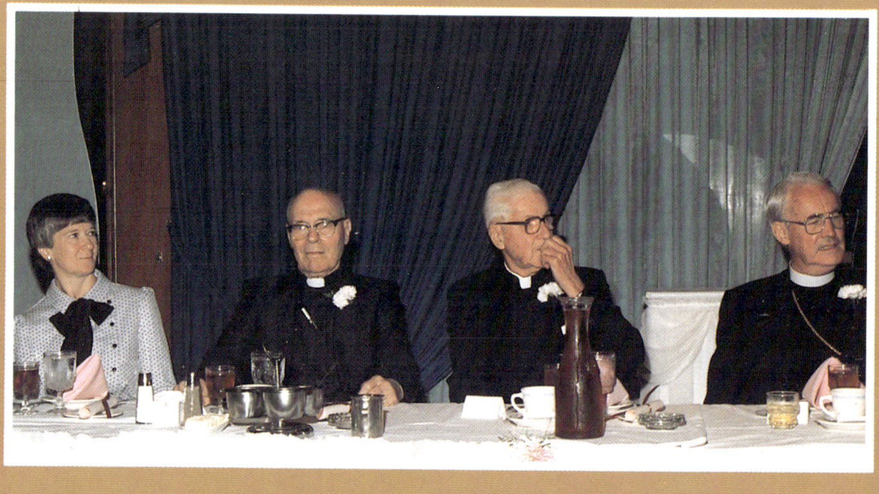

87

88

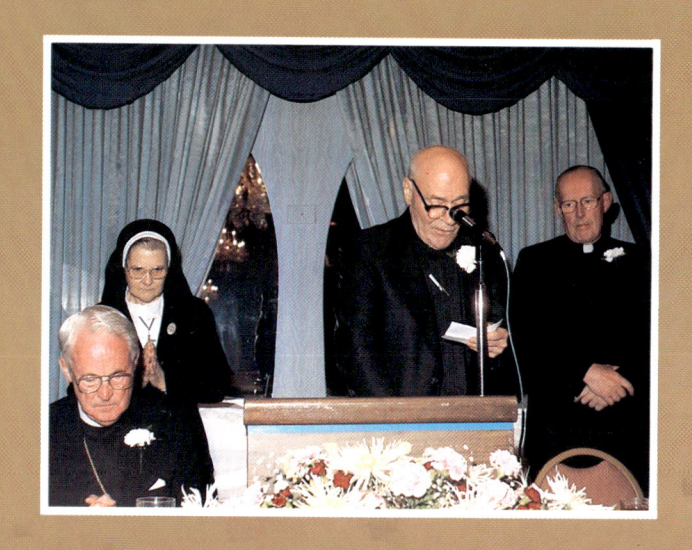

89

90

91

Photos courtesy of Adorne and Rosario Studio.

The following is a list of those who presented one or more of the new Stations of the Cross to the parish:

I	Station	Gift of the Altar and Rosary Society.
II	Station	In Memory of J.O. and M. Palluck.
III	Station	Gift of Mr. and Mrs. P. McDonough.
IV	Station	Gift of Mr. and Mrs. C.J. Ward and Family.
V	Station	In Memory of Mrs. Anna DeMilio from Julia Cernicky.
VI	Station	Gift of Mrs. Margaret Hauslein.
VII	Station	In Memory of Mrs. Winitred and John Kelly.
VIII	Station	Gift of Mrs. Hattie Rambert and Mrs. G. Puccinelli.
IX	Station	Gift of Mr. and Mrs. T.W. Lietz.
X	Station	Gift of Mr. and Mrs. T.W. Lietz.
XI	Station	Gift of Mr. and Mrs. Victor Koster.
XII	Station	In Memory of Cornelius and Hannah Ward.
XIII	Station	Gift of Mr. and Mrs. Walter Borowski.
XIV	Station	In Memory of James Francis Stahl from Sister Mary Francis, O.S.F.

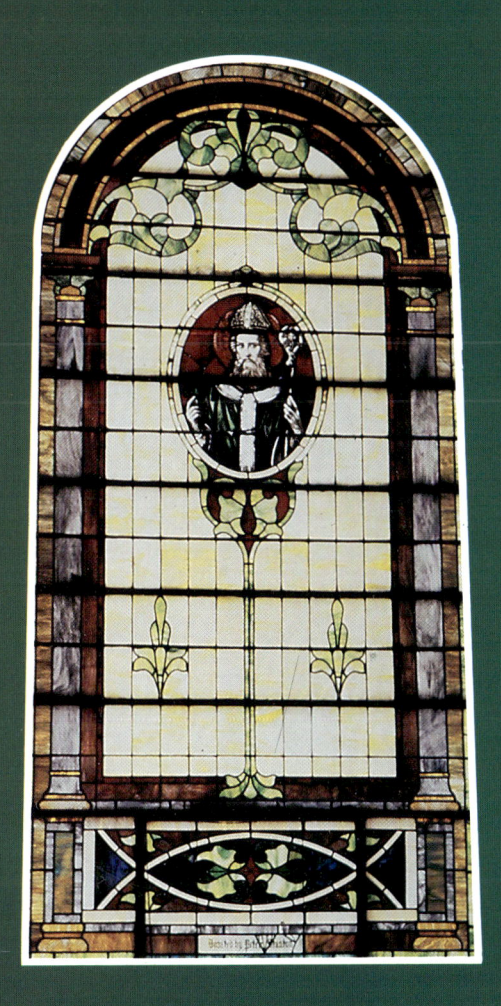

Window depicting Saint Patrick dedicated to Peter Stanton.

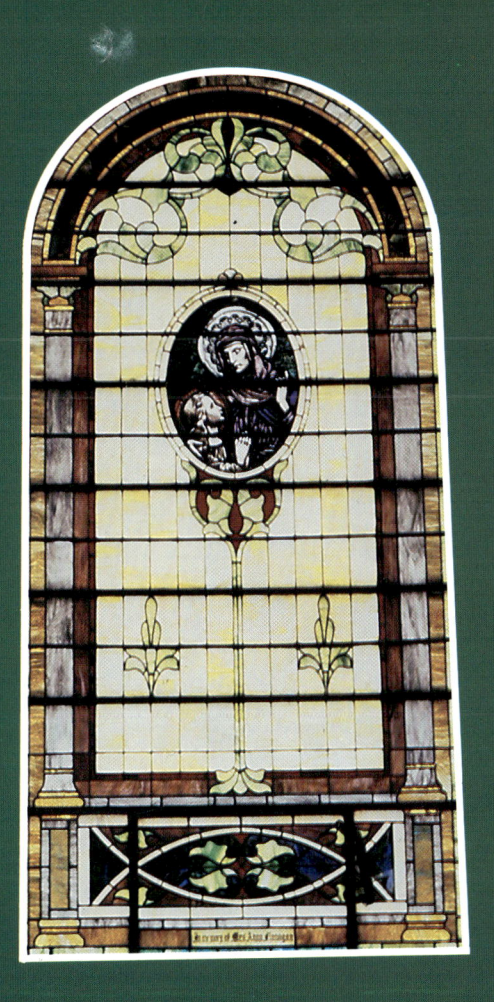

Illustration of Saint Ann — dedicated to Mrs. Anna Flanagan.

Portrait of Our Lady of Sorrows — dedicated to Mrs. Prichard.

Depiction of Christ the Good Shepherd — dedicated to Mrs. Catherine Dunleavy.

Portrayal of Saint Barbara — dedicated to Louis Muller and wife.

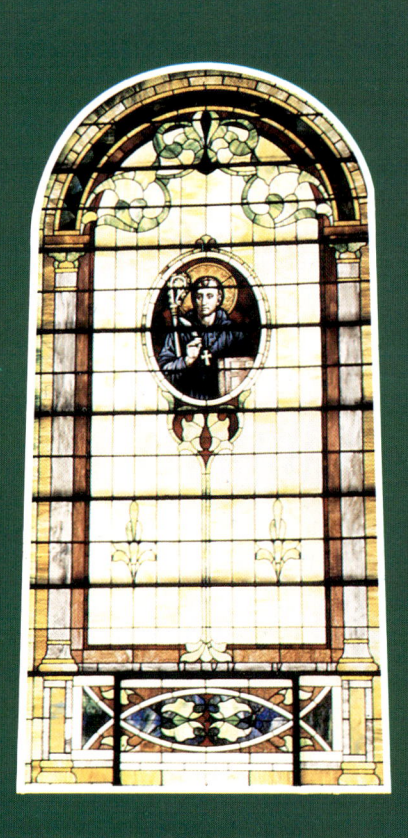

Likeness of Saint Bonaventure — dedicated to Clinton Uller.

Image of St. Mary Magdalene — dedicated to Deceased Servicemen.

Illustrative picture of Saint Thomas Aquinas — dedicated to Dennis and Mary Ellen Ryan.

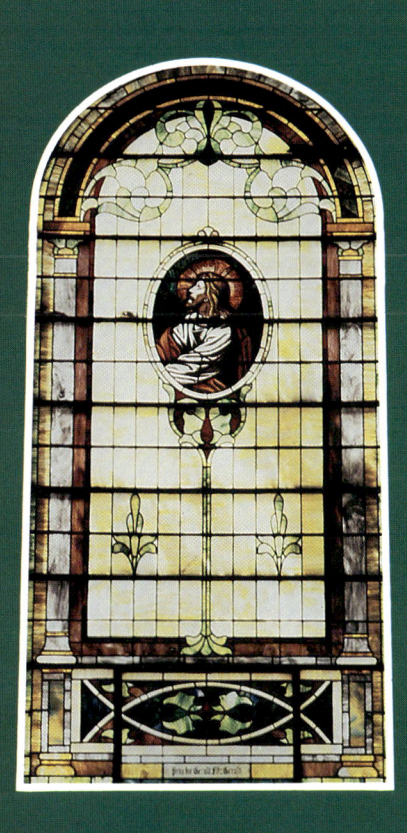

Representation of Agony in the Garden — dedicated to Gerald Fitzgerald.

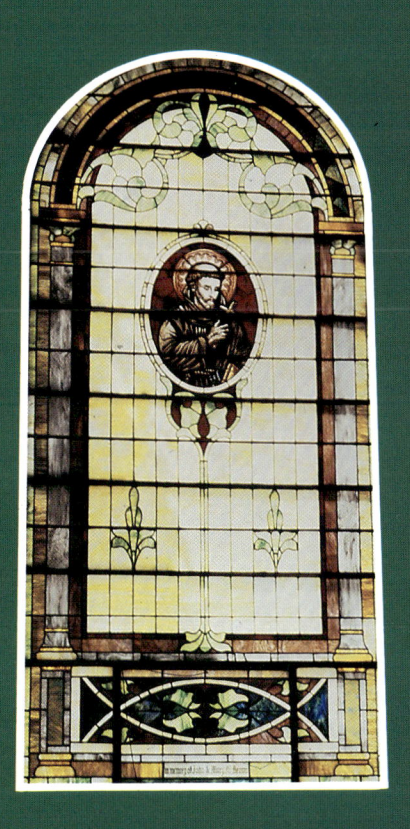

Resemblance of Saint Francis of Assisi — dedicated to John and Mary McKeown.

Portrait of Saint Joseph holding the Christ Child — dedicated to Thomas Biggins and John Thomas Ward.

Image of Sacred Heart of Jesus — dedicated to Rev. Martin J. McGuire.

Depiction of Immaculate Heart of Mary — dedicated to Kathryn Abbott.

Conclusion

Seventy-five years ago two events occurred that would have lasting impact on world history — the first was international — the appearance of Halley's Comet; the second was national, the dedication of the Statue of Liberty. Simultaneously the Parish of Saint Bonaventure was founded.

Providentially over the years, Saint Bonaventure embodied the greatness of these two events. The Comet's fiery pilgrimage across the universe radiated new visions while Ms. Liberty opened its heart to the masses.

Our Parish has been a beacon summoning the poor and underprivileged to its welcoming arms.

As waves of Irish, Italian and other immigrants swept into Deering of International Harvester, Stewart Warner, Terra Cotta and other industrial complexes, Saint Bonaventure was always present offering a better way of life, seeking, decent housing, superior schooling, justice and decency of the work place. The labor programs, youth activities, Christian family movements, prayer groups, affirmed its mission of service. Through the Depression, it gave material help to the disposed, summer camps to the youth, aided in the erection of the massive Lathrop and Senior citizens housing and furnished work for the unemployed.

During the 40's no single Church gave proportionally to the war effort so much of its youth. The parish always conscious of its mission, kept in contact with service people everywhere in the world — providing news from home, religious items, rosaries, prayer books and medals. Those back home were involved with USO, Red Cross and a variety of other patriotic endeavors.

Diligent to the ideas of its patron saint, the parish responded to the population increase by erecting additional school facilities and hiring more teachers.

During these later years vernacular liturgies and schooling made transition easier for our Spanish community.

As we enter the next twenty-five years, new challenges of gentrification, factory closings, uprooting of the poor and lower income await us.

When our patron was a little boy, Saint Francis gave him the name Bonaventure, meaning good fortune. Our wish is that the good fortune which has been our heritage from God these last seventy-five years will continue into the next century.

To our jubilee people and others yet to grace our borders, may the radiant light and welcome arms of Saint Bonaventure Parish offer love, hope and dedicated service.

At the beginning of the creation of nature, our first parents were placed in paradise; but they were driven out by the severity of God's decree because they ate of the forbidden tree. From that time His heavenly mercy has not ceased calling straying man back to the way of penance by giving hope of forgiveness and by promising that a Savior would come. Lest such condescension on God's part should fail to effect our salvation because of ignorance and ingratitude, He never ceased announcing, promising and prefiguring the coming of His Son through the patriarchs, judges, priests, kings and prophets, from Abel to Just to John the Baptist. Through many thousands of years, by many marvelous prophecies He stirred men's minds to faith and inflamed their hearts with living desires.

Finally, the fulness of time had come. The Archangel Gabriel was sent to the Virgin. When she gave her consent to him, the Holy Spirit came upon her like a divine fire inflaming her soul and sanctifying her flesh in perfect purity. But the power of the Most High overshadowed her so that she could endure such fire. By the action of that power, instantly His body was formed, His soul created, and at once both were united to the divinity in the Person of the Son, so that the same Person was God and man, with the properties of each nature maintained.

Oh, if you could feel in some way the quality and intensity of that fire sent from heaven, the refreshing coolness that accompanied it, the consolation it imparted; if you could realize the great exhaltation of the Virgin Mother, the ennobling of the human race, the condescension of the divine majesty; if you could hear the Virgin singing with joy, then I am sure you would sing in sweet tones with the Blessed Virgin that sacred hymn: My soul magnifies the Lord.

From the writings of Saint Bonaventure

THE JOYS OF HEAVEN

Oh, the wonder of this day when all the pains you have patiently borne on earth shall be turned into eternal bliss! Then, with joy flowing from your lips, you will praise the Lord God for all His gifts and say: "The favors of the Lord I will sing forever!"

What a day that shall be for you when Mary the Mother of God will run to meet you; when the Spouse Himself will come with all His saints and say: "Arise, my beloved, my beautiful one, and come! For see, the winter is past, the rains are over and gone."

Sight shall behold the most graceful visions, taste experience the sweetest flavors, odorate perceive the most suave perfumes, touch enfold the most delightful objects, and hearing enjoy the happiest sounds.

Here is eternal soundness. Here you shall be sated with the Lord's glory, and inebriated with the plenty of His house. Here is eternal duration.

There shall be no deformity, weakness, ignorance, or corruption. This shall be the new heaven and the new earth; "there shall be found life without death, youth without aging, joy without sadness, peace without strife, desire without obstacle, light without darkness: an eternal reign perfectly undisturbed."

From the Writings of Saint Bonaventure

WISDOM IS

written in Christ Jesus as in the book of life, in which God the Father has *hidden all the treasures of wisdom and knowledge* (Col. 2:3). Therefore, the only-begotten Son of God, as the uncreated Word, is the book of wisdom and the light that is full of living eternal principles in the mind of the supreme Craftsman, as the inspired Word in the angelic intellects and the blessed, as the incarnate Word in rational minds united with the flesh. Thus throughout the entire kingdom *the manifold wisdom of God* (Eph. 3:10) shines forth from him and in him, as in a mirror containing the beauty of all forms and lights and as in a book in which all things are written according to the deep secrets of God.

O, if only I could find this book
whose origin is eternal,
whose essence is incorruptible,
whose knowledge is life,
whose script is indelible,
whose study is desirable
whose teaching is easy,
whose knowledge is sweet,
whose depth is inscrutable,
whose words are ineffable;
yet all are a single Word!
Truly, whoever finds this book
will *find life and will draw salvation
from the Lord*.

Prayer of Saint Bonaventure

O bountiful Jesus, Your embrace is so sweet, Your touch so pure, Your presence so highly delightful!

O most sweet Jesus, Your embrace sullies not, but purifies; Your touch defiles not, but sanctifies. O Jesus, fountain of all sweetness and delight, how delectable, how good, how joyful, to have Your left hand, Your eternal wisdom and knowledge, under my head, that is, my reason; and to have Your right arm, Your divine mercy and love, embracing my will!

Who could ever experience anything as sweet, pleasing, and delightful as to rest between the arms of such a Spouse, and blissfully to repose in the embrace of such a King, of such a Friend?

But, O Lord God, if these things are so sweet by anticipation, how good they must be when actually tasted! If they are so pleasing to read about, how wonderful will be their actual possession! "O most sweet Jesus, let me taste inwardly through love that which I perceive outwardly through knowledge; make me feel in my heart what I know in my mind."[40]

O Jesus my delight, pierce with the most salutary wound of Your love the very center of my soul, so that it may truly burn, languish, melt, and swoon with the sole desire of You; that it may long to be dissolved, and to abide with You. May it always hunger for You alone, bread of celestial life that came down from heaven; may it thirst for You, fountain of life, source of eternal brightness, torrent of true enjoyment; may it always desire You, search for You, and find You; and may it sweetly rest in You.

Under the reign of Caesar Augustus, the *quiet silence* (Wisd. 18:14) of universal peace had brought such calm to an age which had previously been sorely distressed that through his decree a census of the whole world could be taken. Under the guidance of divine providence, it happened that Joseph, the Virgin's husband, took to the town of Bethlehem the young girl of royal descent who was pregnant. When nine months had passed since his conception, the King of Peace *like a bridegroom from his bridal chamber* (1 Par. 22:9; Ps. 18:6), came forth from the virginal womb. Although he was great and rich, he became small and poor for us. He chose to be born away from a home in a stable, to be wrapped in swaddling clothes, to be nourished by virginal milk and to lie in a manger between an ox and an ass. Then there shone upon us a day of new redemption, restoration of the past and eternal happiness. Then throughout the whole world the heavens became honey-sweet.

Then in your mind
keep the shepherds' watch,
marvel at the assembling host of angels,
join in the heavenly melody,
singing with your voice and heart:
*Glory to God in the highest
and on earth peace
to men of good will.*

From the writings of Saint Bonaventure

Acknowledgements

We would like to acknowledge and thank those individuals who contributed their time and/or talents to the completion and publication of this book:

Pat Bargi
Sr. Bonaventure (Kathleen Hill)
Sr. Charlotte Marie (Margaret Smith)
Derek Crenshaw
Rev. Lucius B. Delire
Norma Ehrenberg
Pat Foley
Rose Foster
Rev. Austin Graff
Robert Graff
Ernest King
Marie Kirschbaum
Al Krauser
LaSalle Photo Company
Sr. Mildred (Jackson)
Gloria Meyer
Rev. Michael J. Murray
Andrew Pescon
Nestor Pescon
John Steiner
Kathy Stubenrauch
Sr. Veronica (Caroline Carmody)

The Parish is most grateful to LaSalle Photo Service for its kind donation of Saint Bonaventure buttons and holy cards. These items augmented the joyfulness of our Jubilee and will be treasured by all our people as precious keepsakes for years to come.

COMPLIMENTS OF LaSALLE PHOTO SERVICE

1700 W. Diversey
Chicago, Illinois

Bibliography

Reference:

Bennett Archambault — "The Origins, Growth and Development of Stewart-Warner Corporation", October 1963.

Edward Baumann and John O'Brien — "Was It Murder" — Sunday — The Chicago Tribune Magazine , August 3, 1986.

Stephen Bedell Clark — "The Lake View Saga," 1974.

Chicago Record, 1897.

Chicago Sun-Times, August 8, 1978.

Chicago Tribune 1897 and 1898.

Chicago Tribune, October 11 and 12, 1911.

International Harvester Company of America — "Roots in Chicago, One Hundred Years Deep" — 1847 to 1947.

Sharon S. Darling — "Chicago Ceramics and Glass" Chicago Historical Society — 1979.

Larry Kohl — "Origin of Earth and Life" — National Geographic, August 1985.

Rand McNally Map of the City of Chicago and Suburbs — 1900.

St. Bonaventure Priests

Martin J. McGuire
Peter Gereghty
Peter Quinn
Henry Weber
William P. Long
Joseph Phelan
Francis Buck
Joseph O'Callaghan
Joseph Carton
Vincent J. Moran
Philip Cahill
Peter Duffy
Eugene Lyons
James Donlan
John Kelly
Peter Riley
Edward Reading
William Sheridan
Francis McGrath
Anthony Gaughan
Edward Conway
Leo P. Coggins
George Helfrich
Lucius B. Delire
James A. Colleran
Thoms Conley
Eugene Faucher
Eugene Parker
John P. Cunningham
Herbert Boesen
Lawrence Malcolm
Stephen Mangan
Thomas A. Moran
Charles Fannelli
Michael J. Murray
Michael J. Boehm
Richard Simon

Priests ordained from St. Bonnie:

Edward Pellicore
James Gaynor
Joseph Morin
Robert Baranowski

MSGR. VINCENT J. MORAN

In loving remembrance of deceased priests, sisters and parishioners of Saint Bonaventure Parish.

Rev. Martin J. McGuire

Rev. Peter J. Geraghty

Rev. Msgr. William P. Long

Rev. Peter Quinn

Rev. Henry Weber

Rev. Anthony Gaughan

Rev. Peter J. Riley

Rev. Herbert Boesen

Rev. Philip T. Cahill

Rev. Joseph Phelan

Rev. Joseph O'Callaghan

Rev. Francis J. Buck

Rev. Peter F. Duffy

Rev. Edward J. Reading

May the angels lead you into paradise; may the martyrs come to welcome you on your way and lead you into the heavenly city, Jerusalem.

May the choir of angels welcome you and with Lazarus who once was poor, may you have everlasting rest.

DIAMOND SUBSCRIBERS

COTTER AND COMPANY

Congratulations on your Diamond Jubilee

COUNCIL OF CATHOLIC WOMEN

Congratulations! Officers: Pres. Bernice Schlapinski, 1st V.P. Gerry Peterson, 2nd V.P. Beverly Battiste, Sec. Norma Ehrenberg, Treas. Tecla Monahan

ITALIAN CATHOLIC FEDERATION
Saint Bonaventure Parish

Congratulations and best wishes

REVEREND LUCIUS B. DELIRE

LAWRENCE FRATESCHI FAMILY — OLGA, ELLEN AND LARRY

Give us the spirit of your comfort. Best wishes for another 75 years.

REVEREND MONSIGNOR VINCENT J. MORAN

REVEREND MICHAEL J. MURRAY

STEWART-WARNER CORPORATION
Alemite and Instrument Division

Congratulations to the people of Saint Bonaventure on the occasion of your 75th Anniversary from your neighbor in our 80th year

MR. AND MRS. ROY ROHTER AND TERRY

REVEREND WILLIAM D. RYAN, JAMES J. RYAN and FAMILY, MARGARET RYAN VIRTUE and FAMILY, AND MARIE J.F. RYAN

Congratulations to Saint Bonaventure Parish in memory of Denny and Mayme O'Connor Ryan

PATRICK KELLEY

MURRAY FAMILY

In loving memory of Michael and Frances Murray

GOLD SUBSCRIBERS

ASTRO AMUSEMENT COMPANY, INC.

Our best wishes to all the members of Saint Bonaventure Parish during this very special year. God bless you.

MR. AND MRS. PAUL BATTISTE AND BEVERLY

Best wishes on the 75th Jubilee of Saint Bonaventure Parish.

MAE CARPENTER

EWALD FUNERAL HOME

The Ewald-Barlock Family has been fortunate in being able to share these 75 years at Saint Bonaventure Church. Our best wishes are that this association continue.

A FRIEND

REVEREND CHARLES FANELLI

God Bless you on your 75th. I will never forget your kindness during my 7 years with you.

MARY KUNZ

REVEREND LAWRENCE J. MALCOLM

Thank you for your kindness and support during my "rookie" years in the priesthood. I received much more than I gave! God bless you.

SCHNAKENBERG ACE HARDWARE

Congratulations on the 75th Year of your continuing service to the community doing God's work.

SILVER SUBSCRIBERS

ATLAS ELEVATOR COMPANY

ST. BEDE THE VENERABLE PARISH
Best wishes

MRS. ELLEN BONINI
In memory of my husband, Albert

MR. AND MRS. RALPH J. FOLEY
Congratulations to the people of Saint Bonaventure Parish on this happy occasion. You are great!

REVEREND JAMES G. GAYNOR

VIOLA GORMAN
Congratulations and God bless Saint Bonaventure parishioners

REVEREND WILLIAM GUBBINS

MRS. ELSIE HUBECK
Congratulations to Saint Bonaventure Parish on its 75th Diamond Jubilee

SAINT JOSAPHAT CHURCH
Best wishes on your 75th year from the People and Priests of Saint Josaphat Church

JOSEPH AND SUE KUNZ
Forty-five year parishioners

A FRIEND

BOB McCANN HEATING
Congratulations and may there be 75 more.

McWHINNEY B.A.
From your neighbors and parishioners for the past 75 years — McWhinney B.A.

ARMANDO AND FLORENCE PAGNUCCI
Congratulations! for the fond memories and spiritual help given to our families

SILVER SUBSCRIBERS

MR. AND MRS. EDWARD J. O'CONNOR

BERNICE RAMBERT
Best eight years of my life were spent at Saint Bonaventure Parochial School 1924-1931

SAINT RAYMOND CHURCH
Prayerful good wishes from the Community of Saint Raymond

MR. AND MRS. NICHOLAS ROSCH
From 1938-1985 were the happiest years we spent at Saint Bonaventure parish

CONGRESSMAN DAN ROSTENKOWSKI and ALDERMAN TERRY GABINSKI
Best wishes on your Diamond Jubilee

MR. AND MRS. EDWARD STEINER AND FAMILY
Congratulations and best wishes

RAYMOND STUBENRAUCH
Thank you for seventy-five years.

SAINT THERESA PARISH, PALATINE
Congratulations from your friends at Saint Theresa Parish

MR. AND MRS. EUGENE TOSSI
Congratulations on your Diamond Jubilee Year.

MR. AND MRS. DANIEL VALDEZ and family
Congratulations! Thanks for the memories

A FRIEND
Thanks for everything

THE CHILDREN OF ALICE AND JOSEPH STOPA WITH LOVE:
JOHN, JOSEPH, ROBERT, ROBERTA, BERNADINE AND RAYMOND STOPA

BENEFACTORS

SAINT ALPHONSUS CHURCH

ASHLAND ADDISON FLORIST COMPANY

MR. AND MRS. WILLIAM BARGI

LUCILLE BOBRYTZKE

SAINT CONSTANCE CHURCH

P. BARSI SONS FUNERAL DIRECTORS

LEO M. BRIESKE & SON FUNERAL HOME

REVEREND BOB BURNELL

REVEREND EDWIN M. CONWAY

DIVINE INFANT CHURCH

REVEREND JAMES DONLAN

THE EHRENBERG FAMILY

FRANCES GECKS

MR. AND MRS. BRANDINO GIANNONI & FAMILY

REVEREND JOSEPH A. GRAFF

ELLEN T. GROSCH

AMANDA AND MARLENE GUNTHER

JANE, ART AND JOSEPH HITTERMAN

MR. AND MRS. GEORGE KASPER

REVEREND JOSEPH O. KING

KIRSCHBAUM FAMILY

LAKE VIEW TRUST & SAVINGS BANK

SAINT LEONARD CHURCH

MR. AND MRS. STAN LINDMEIER

MONSIGNOR EUGENE F. LYONS

ANGELINE MARKIEWICZ AND FAMILY

MR. AND MRS. WILLIE MARTINEZ AND FAMILY

MARY AND JOSEPH CIRCLE

VERA MAZZANTI

HELEN McBREEN

SAINT JOHN NEPOMUCENE PARISH/SPRED

PATRICK J. McDERMOTT

RUSSELL J. McKAY FAMILY

GLORIA MEYER

HARRIET MISCHKE

MUELHOEFER'S LAKE VIEW CHAPEL

GARRY AND MARY NOONAN

MR. AND MRS. FRANCIS ORTMANN AND FAMILY

OUR LADY OF THE BROOK CHURCH

MR. AND MRS. GIAMPIERO PACINI

JOSEPHINE PELLEGRINI AND FAMILY

R.F. PICKEN, PEERLESS CONFECTION

REVEREND MONSIGNOR EDWARD M. PELLICORE

SAINT JOSEPH CHURCH, SUMMIT

MR. AND MRS. HARRY PRATO

SACRED HEART CHURCH, PALOS HILLS

MRS. MARY SCHWARTZ

REVEREND WILLIAM H. SHERIDAN

SPANISH HOSPITALITY COMMITTEE
Saint Bonaventure Parish

CHRIS AND ROSALIE SCHMIDT

KATHLEEN STUBENRAUCH

MRS. MARGARET TANNER

A FRIEND

TRANSILWRAP COMPANY, INC.

REVEREND RICHARD J. FELLER

Sponsors

SAINT ADRIAN PARISH

SAINT ALBERT THE GREAT PARISH

SAINT ANNE PARISH

SAINT AMBROSE PARISH

CATHERINE APPELHANS

ASH MANOR RESTAURANT

MR. AND MRS. MARIO BARGI

SAINT BARNABAS PARISH

LOUIS BATTISTE FAMILY

ANNE AND DOUGLAS BASCHIERE

BRAUN ENTERPRISES, INC.

BROOKLINE SHADE COMPANY

CANFIELD'S BEVERAGES

ANGELO CARLI

AUGUSTINO CIUCCI FAMILY

THOMAS FRANCIS CREELY

FRANK DAWSON

DIVINE SAVIOR PARISH

MR. AND MRS. RAYMOND G. DOLGOPOL

MR. AND MRS. RICHARD L. ELWART

REVEREND JOHN F. FAHEY

LORETTA SULLIVAN FRISCH

MR. AND MRS. ANTHONY GALLINA

MR. AND MRS. ELIO GEMIGNANI

MARGARET D. GOLM

SAINT HELEN CHURCH

MS. PATRICIA HITZSCHKE

MRS. E. JANKOSKI

ANN AND JOHN KANNADY

KOCH COMPANY, INC.

ELIZABETH LACH

CELESTE LAVELLI

EUGENIA LAVELLI

MR. AND MRS. ALBERT MARCHINI

SAINT MARGARET MARY PARISH

VERNA MARTINE

SAINT MARY OF THE ASSUMPTION PARISH

SAINT MARY OF THE WOODS PARISH

REVEREND LEONARD H. MATTEI

REVEREND MATTHEW McDONALD

REVEREND ROBERT F. McGINNITY

EILEEN McNULTY

MET DISPLAY AND FIXTURE

SAM AND TECLA MONAHAN

MOTHER OF GOD PARISH

MR. AND MRS. DENNIS P. NERI

MR. AND MRS. GENO NERI

PATRICIA COSTELLO OPPELS, FLORENCE COSTELLO AND MICHAEL COSTELLO

THE PARISHIONERS AND STAFF OF OUR LADY OF HOPE CHURCH

DENNIS PALLUCK

MR. AND MRS. ALFRED PAOLI

LOUISE PAVEGLIO

REVEREND RAYMOND A. PAVIS

MRS. LESLIE PETERSON

ANGELO PIERUCCI

SAINT PIUS X PARISH

MRS. MARTHA RANACHOWSKI

RICHARD'S PACKING COMPANY

ROCKWELL FAMILY

MR. AND MRS. ERALDO SIMONETTI & SON

SAINT SYLVESTER PARISH

SAINT TERESA OF AVILA PARISH

MR. AND MRS. CHESTER J. WALEN

MARY P. WATTS

MR. AND MRS. JOHN WURBIA

A FRIEND

SAINT ZACHARY PARISH

MR. AND MRS. WALTER F. ZADROZNY

A FRIEND

Patrons

VIRGINIA ABBOTT
REVEREND RAYMOND J. ACKERMAN
REVEREND MICHAEL J. ADAMS
MARY AHERN
MARGARET AHERN
ANN ALESSE
SAINT ANDREW PARISH
HEINRICH ARCH
MR. AND MRS. LOUIS A. BASSI
JEANETTE BAUMANN
MR. AND MRS. FRED BECKER, JR.
MR. AND MRS. MARIO BERTOLANI
JOSEPH BIEGUN
JOSEPHINE F. BIENIAS
REVEREND R. PETER BOWMAN
BRAVO PIZZA, INC.
JEFFREY G. BRAY
FLORENCE A. BROCIEK
JOAN AND WILLIAM BROWN
MRS. CHARLES BUCHMILLER
STEVEN AND BERNICE BUSH
ROBERT CARDILLO
ANN CAWLEY
SAINT CELESTINE PARISH
MR. AND MRS. TILMON CHELETTE
CHICAGO WALDORF SCHOOL
REVEREND JAMES A. COLLERAN
MR. AND MRS. MARSHALL COLOMBANI
REVEREND THOMAS P. CONLEY
SANTIAGO CORREA
REVEREND VINCENT F. COSTELLO
MR. AND MRS. WILLIAM CUMMINGS
REVEREND RAYMOND L. CUSACK
PETRA DEL VALLE
MR. AND MRS. JOHN DORSCH
DOLORES HAYES DOUGLAS
MR. AND MRS. RAYMOND DOWNES
REVEREND SYLVESTER DUDZINSKI
WANDA DZIUBA
MONSIGNOR JOHN J. EGAN
MRS. VERONICA EGELKRAUT
MS. HELEN C. EWALD
JOSEPH J. EWALD FUNERAL HOME
MARY DeZETTER FAIRFIELD
AGNES FALTUM
JOSEPHINE FANUCCHI
REVEREND JOHN FEARON
DR. AND MRS. DENO J. FENILI
MR. AND MRS. CARLO FINI
JOHN FINLEY
REVEREND EDWARD P. FITZGERALD
GUMERCINDA FLORES
BERENICE FLOSI
EILEEN AND JAY FONTANETTA
ROSEMARY FOSTER

ANNE FOY
SAINT FRANCIS XAVIER PARISH
JOE AND BARBARA FRANK
ESTELLE GABEL
MRS. FRANK GALASHINSKI
MARGARET GALUHN
WINIFRED GANNON
AGNES F. GAYNOR
JAMES P. GEBBIA
MARGARET GLOWIENKE
JAMES P. GORMAN
JOSEPH R. GORMAN, JR.
DALE AND GEORGETTE GREENE
HELEN GRENKOWITZ
ROSE MARIE GRZESZCZAK
MR. AND MRS. MARIO GUGLIOTTA
ANNE HENNIGAN HARTNETT
REVEREND RICHARD L. HILLS
HOLY NAME OF MARY PARISH
REVEREND JOSEPH HUDIK
MR. AND MRS. THOMAS HUGHES
IMMACULATE CONCEPTION PARISH (North Park Ave.)
REVEREND MICHAEL JACOBSEN
REVEREND PIERCE J. JOYCE
SAINT JULIE PARISH
MR. AND MRS. BERNARD KACKERT
REVEREND JOHN M. KANE
LYDIA AND NORBERT KAZIK
REVEREND JAMES W. KEATING
REVEREND FRANCIS J. KELPSAS
REVEREND JOHN G. KLEIN
M.I. KILGALLON
ELAINE KNIGHT
REVEREND MONSIGNOR HARRY C. KOENIG
EVELYN SYCHOWSKI KOLAKOWSKI
JOHN KOLLER
MR. AND MRS. JOHN KOSOVICH
FRANK KOTT
JEANETTE D. KULANDA
EMILY D. KUNZ
MR. AND MRS. RAYMOND KUNZ
CHET AND PEGGY KULIS
MR. AND MRS. ELMER LANDINI
LORRAINE LANDRY
FLORA K. LANG
HELEN V. LANG
THERESA LAPETINA
SAINT LAWRENCE O'TOOLE PARISH
MURPHY & JONES CO., INC.
MRS. MARTIN LENIHAN
NORMA LITZ
REVEREND LEO J. LYONS
REVEREND PATRICK M. LYONS
FRED AND DOROTHY MAGNANENSI

Patrons

EDITH M. MAHER
REVEREND ROBERT G. MAIR
MRS. C. MALCZEWSKI & FAMILY
SAINT MARK PARISH
MARK & JOHN'S RESTAURANT
MARION H. MARTIUS
JOHN AND RON MAZIARKA
SARAH McDERMOTT
EUGENE P. McDONOUGH
ANNIE McHALE
REVEREND GEORGE McKENNA
REVEREND THOMAS S. McMAHON
PAUL MELLENTHIN FAMILY
MARGARET MENNELLA
MR. AND MRS. ROY METCALF, JR.
MONSIGNOR CHARLES N. METER
MRS. NORMAN M. MERTES
MRS. FRED MEYER
MR. AND MRS. EDWARD MILLER
MRS. GEORGE MILLER
THE MISHKE FAMILY
VICTORIA C. MITTAGE
REVEREND JAMES E. MORRISSEY
MARY K. MOTSCH
REVEREND JOHN M. MURPHY
REVEREND EDWARD F. MYERS
MR. AND MRS. FRANK NATALE
MRS. ROSE A. NEUMAN
REVEREND JOHN J. NICOLA
ALVIN W. NITSCH
NOTTOLINI FAMILY
REVEREND MONSIGNOR THOMAS OBRYCKI
REVEREND JAMES J. O'BRIEN
MR. AND MRS. CLARENCE OSIECKI
MR. AND MRS. ROBERT P. OKEN
HENRY AND LEONA ORTH
LEA PAOLI
SETTIMA PAPUCCI
ROSE ANN NEUMAN PARCHIM
NELLA PARENTI
ELIO AND VALENTINE PAPUCCI
JOSEPHINE PASQUINELLI
MARTHA PATOCK AND FAMILY
SAINT PAUL OF THE CROSS PARISH
ANDY AND EMILIE PECSON
MR. AND MRS. THOMAS L. PELS
MR. ROBERT PETERSON
REVEREND JOSEPH A. PHELAN
AGNES PLOTZKE
MR. AND MRS. EDWARD POPPENGA
NESTOR PRATO FAMILY
MR. AND MRS. ALBERT PRIAMI
REVEREND FRANCIS PHELAN
DOROTHY REGINETZ

REMER COPIERS & OFFICE SUPPLIES
JOSEPH AND KATHERINE RIEBANDT
ROSE RIDOLFI
ALICE AND HARRY ROHDE
TITO ROMAN
NICHOLAS C. ROSCH
REVEREND JOHN C. ROSEMEYER
REVEREND PAUL F. ROSEMEYER
EDWARD AND HELEN ROSZKOWSKI
EDWARD RUTA FAMILY
FLORENCE BARTOLOMEI ROSELLI
BEATRICE SANTOYO
MARY AND PATRICIA SASS
REVEREND FRANCIS G. SCANLAN
MARY ANN SCHANIT
ROBERT AND REGINA SCHATTNIK
PAULINE SCHIMMEL
THE SCHLAPINSKI FAMILY
REVEREND J. SCHMEIER
MR. AND MRS. OTTO R. SCHOENBERG
ARLENE F. SCHWARZKOPF
SAINT RAPHAEL PARISH
REVEREND DEAN F. SEMMER
MR. AND MRS. SAL SETTIPANE, SR.
REVEREND ROBERT J. SHANNON
REVEREND WILLIAM J. SHERIDAN
DARIA SKIBICKI
THE STANEK FAMILY
LEE STANLEY, THE ANTIQUE STORE
REVEREND WALTER STEFANSKI
MR. AND MRS. JAMES STONE
MRS. ALICE R. STOPA
JOSEPH S. STOPA
RAYMOND F. STOPA
ROBERTA J. STOPA
MRS. JOSEPH SUCH
MR. AND MRS. JOHN SZAFRANSKI
THE TRAVEN FAMILY
REVEREND PATRICK TUCKER
SAINT TURIBIUS PARISH
MICHAEL F. UDROW
MR. AND MRS. WILBUR UDROW & FAMILY
BERNICE AND WILLIAM UDROW
REVEREND KENNETH VELO
MARGUERITE HENNIGAN WAGNER
LESTER AND ROSEANNE WALLINGFORD
MR. AND MRS. ALEX WEIGEL
LORRAINE M. WIERZBICKI
MR. AND MRS. RAY WILSON
CARL AND LEONA WIRTZ
MRS. KATHERINE WITT
REVEREND PETER M. YANGAS
THERESA YUZA AND FAMILY
ZUM DEUTSCHEN ECK

IN MEMORIAM

Deceased	Requested by
Sgt. John McFarland	Josephine Pellegrini
Mr. and Mrs. Edmond Roberts	Josephine Pellegrini
The Marcotte Family	Josephine Pellegrini
The Roberts Family	Josephine Pellegrini
The Pellegrini Family	Josephine Pellegrini
Pia and Nello Bargi	Louis Bargi
Helen Schauer	Peggy Wells and Maureen Marcisz
Mr. and Mrs. Angelo Bertolani	Mr. and Mrs. Mario Bertolani
Mr. and Mrs. Paul Herman	Edward Roszkowski Family
Mr. and Mrs. J. Roszkowski	Edward Roszkowski Family
Sgt. John McFarland	Mrs. Ellen McFarland
Deceased of Malczewski Family	Mrs. C. Malczewski
Deceased of Chappa Family	Mrs. C. Malczewski
Otello Bargi	Mary Bargi,
Raymond Schlapinski	Wife and children
John Koller	Family
Anthony and Dusolina Bartolomei	Florence B. Roselli, daughter
Harold Bartolomei	Florence B. Roselli, sister
Harry Rakowski	Mr. and Mrs. Daniel Valdez
Edward Rakowski	Ms. Debra A. Pietrzak
Mary Kasin	Clarence Kasin, Jr.
Mr. and Mrs. John Dolgopol	Mr. and Mrs. Raymond G. Dolgopol
David DeZetter Family	Nell D. Mertes

IN MEMORIAM

Deceased	Requested by
Nicholas J. Meyer	Gloria Meyer
Mr. and Mrs. Jacob Meyer	Gloria Meyer
Mr. and Mrs. Amedeo Sisi	Gloria Meyer
Mr. and Mrs. Paul Marchini	Gloria Meyer
Mr. and Mrs. Frank Karl, Sr.	Mrs. Leslie Peterson
Mr. and Mrs. Walter Karl	Mrs. Leslie Peterson
Robert E. Peterson	Mrs. Leslie Peterson
Leslie E. Peterson	Mrs. Leslie Peterson
Sophie Karl	Mrs. Leslie Peterson
Ulysses Grant Hill	Genevieve W. Hill
Mr. and Mrs. Frank Marsalek	Mr. and Mrs. Alex Weigel
Mr. and Mrs. Stanley Marsalek	Mr. and Mrs. Alex Weigel
Mr. and Mrs. Caspar Weigel	Mr. and Mrs. Alex Weigel
John Lusak	Mrs. John Lusak
Frank Marsalek Family	Mrs. John Lusak
Lusak Family	Mrs. John Lusak
Gene Jankoski	Mary Jankoski
Mr. and Mrs. J. Jankoski	Mary Jankoski
Mr. and Mrs. John Wlodarczak	Isabelle Kotruch, daughter
James J. McDermott	Sarah McDermott
Michael J. Richards	Mary Richards
Mr. and Mrs. Patrick Maher	Mary Buchmiller
Charles Buchmiller	Mary Buchmiller
Joseph Maher	Edith Maher

IN MEMORIAM

Deceased	Requested by
Thomas O. Sansone, Sr.	Irene Sansone
Mr. and Mrs. Joseph Hebel	Bernice Hebel
Anthony Tossi	Wife
George Tossi	Family
Joseph Ruta	Family
Ernest G. Giltner	Minnie Giltner
Charles and Julia Gallet	Children, Ernie Gallet, Mary and Lillian Hughes
Thomas R. Hughes	Lillian Hughes
Mr. and Mrs. Edward Udrow	William Udrow
Peter C. Motsch	Mary K. Motsch
Nicholas Motsch	Mary K. Motsch
Katherine Sweeney	Mary K. Motsch
Rev. Vincent Walsh, C.M.	Mary K. Motsch
Margaret Uzdrowski	Mary Ann Schanit
Mr. and Mrs. Robert Dawson	Children
Armenio and Emma Priami	Mr. and Mrs. Albert Priami
John and Lottie Gorski	Mr. and Mrs. Albert Priami
Paul and Jane Ruda	Mr. and Mrs. Albert Priami
Alexander Reginetz	Dorothy and Doug Reginetz
James F. Kosovich	Mr. and Mrs. John Kosovich
Mr. and Mrs. Stanley Kurek	Mr. and Mrs. John Trzebny, Jr.
Mr. and Mrs. John Trzebny, Sr.	Mr. and Mrs. John Trzebny, Jr.

IN MEMORIAM

Deceased	Requested by
Mr. and Mrs. Joseph Palluck	Mr. and Mrs. Mario Bargi
Mr. and Mrs. James Fredian	Mr. and Mrs. Mario Bargi
Mr. and Mrs. Frank Fredian	Mr. and Mrs. Mario Bargi
Marie Palluck	Mr. and Mrs. Mario Bargi
Virginia and Victor Lavelli	Lavelli Family
Natalina Pucci	Mr. and Mrs. John Foster and Family
Celestino Bartolomei	Mrs. Egitina Bartolomei
Elma Finley	John Finley
Mr. and Mrs. Jacob Frank	Catherine Appelhans
Mr. and Mrs. Jacob Appelhans	Catherine Appelhans
Adam Appelhans	Catherine Appelhans
John Frank	Catherine Appelhans
Mrs. Mary Bartel	Catherine Appelhans
Peter Watts	Mary Watts
Mr. and Mrs. John Mackowicz	Mary Watts
Mr. and Mrs. Peter Szwabinski	Mary Watts
Mr. and Mrs. Xavier Awsiuk	Mary Watts
Mr. and Mrs. Nickolaus Kasarewski	Mary Watts
Thaddius W. Brociek	Family
Fred C. Meyer	Harriet Meyer
Joseph R. Gorman	Viola M. Gorman
Leona McCann	Viola M. Gorman
James and Mary Gorman	Jim Gorman
2/c John P. Gorman, U.S.N.	V.M. Gorman

IN MEMORIAM

Deceased	Requested by
Leo Ranachowski	Mr. and Mrs. Dennis P. Neri
William A. Tanner	Margaret Tanner
Edward F. Seebacher	Seebacher Family
Mr. and Mrs. Nick Funck	Seebacher Family
Mr. and Mrs. George Seebacher	Seebacher Family
Anthony J. Kunz	Mr. and Mrs. Joseph Kunz
Mr. and Mrs. Frank Kasteiner	Mr. and Mrs. Joseph Kunz
Rita Landini	Mr. and Mrs. Eraldo Simonetti and Son
Clarence Laxner	A. Laxner Family
Edwin Laxner	A. Laxner Family
Anne Laxner	A. Laxner Family
Sister M. Pauline, C.S.J.	Jane Lohrmann Hitterman
James Cawley	Mrs. Ann Cawley
Deceased Members of Szafranski Family	Miss Theresa Szafranski
Ellen E. Powers	Ellen C. Powers
Pauline and Ernest Jones	Mr. and Mrs. D. Baschiere
Fran and Frank Berger	Mr. and Mrs. D. Baschiere
James Baschiere	Mr. and Mrs. D. Baschiere
Florence Jensen	Mr. and Mrs. D. Baschiere
Earl and Anna Lenz	Nestor and Dolores Prato
Bianca Paoli	Lea and Alfred Paoli
Joseph Paoli	Lea and Alfred Paoli
Mr. and Mrs. Ernest J. Jones	Rose Wallingford
Andrew Faltum	Family

IN MEMORIAM

Deceased	Requested by
Geno J. Fanucchi	Josephine Fanucchi
Giacinto Brogi	Josephine Fanucchi
Oreste Papucci	Settima Papucci
Henry Plotzke	Wife
Alfred Pasquinelli	Josephine Pasquinelli
Peter Saisi	Josephine Pasquinelli
Mr. and Mrs. Aladino Saisi	Josephine Pasquinelli
Leonard Novak	Mary Novak
Mr. and Mrs. G. Gabriel and Sons	Mary Novak and Anne Gabriel
Anthony R. Gabriel	Anne Gabriel
Mr. and Mrs. Peter Guerra	Mary Novak
Mr. and Mrs. John Natali	Anne Gabriel
Joseph Stopa, Sr.	Family
Mr. and Mrs. Jacob Frank	Joe Frank
Gino and Isola Vettori	Armando and Florence Pagnucci
Dario Pagnucci	Armando and Florence Pagnucci
Mr. and Mrs. George Seebacher	Mr. and Mrs. Dale Greene
Mrs. Augusta Oken	Mr. and Mrs. Robert Oken
Mr. and Mrs. Raymond Oken	Mr. and Mrs. Robert Oken
Mr. and Mrs. George Hayes	Hayes Family
Mrs. Martha Lackowski	Mr. and Mrs. E. Miller
John and Leta Martin	Florence and Eileen
Delmo J. Ciucci	Regina Ciucci

IN MEMORIAM

Deceased	Requested by
Mr. and Mrs. Romolo Neri	Mr. and Mrs. Geno Neri
Mr. and Mrs. Gaetano Maita	Mr. and Mrs. Geno Neri
Astolfo Ridolfi	Rose Ridolfi
Jesse Knight	Elaine Knight
Theresa Moroske	Elaine Knight
Mamie Blaul	Elaine Knight
Rose and Anthony Tossi, Sr.	Daughters and Son
Lawrence J. Tossi	Sisters and Brother
Deceased of Abbott Family	Virginia Abbott
Mackowicz Family	Walen Family
Deceased of Walen Family	Walen Family
Deceased of Capelik Family	Walen Family
Deceased of Labac Family	Walen Family
Frank Maninfior	Laura Maninfior
Diane Plamas	James Plamas
Rose Bernd	Frances Bernd
Alex Bernd, Sr.	Frances Bernd
Marie Barts	Lawrence Barts
G.H. Barts	Lawrence Barts
Anthony Lach, Sr.	Elizabeth Lach
Mr. and Mrs. Joe Lach	Elizabeth Lach
Mr. and Mrs. Mike Kaczmaryk	Elizabeth Lach
Mr. and Mrs. Stanley Cudecki	Elizabeth Lach
Charles H. McNulty	Mary McNulty
George and Genevieve Hebel	Hebel Family

IN MEMORIAM

Deceased	Requested by
Mr. and Mrs. Angelo Landini	Elmer Landini
Mr. and Mrs. Fred Struck	Harriet Landini
Julia Pokornowski	Mr. and Mrs. Albert Jancovic
Theresa Grupenhagen	Marie Zilka
John and Mary Krystyniak	Daughter, Sophie
Evelyn Smidl	Parents
Steve Hubeck	Mrs. Elsie Hubeck, wife
Joseph Purzinec	Mrs. Elsie Hubeck, daughter
Mrs. Emilia Pruzinec	Mrs. Elsie Hubeck, daughter
Mrs. Elizabeth Zigmond	Mrs. Elsie Hubeck, sister
Fred J. Kunz	Family
William P. Glowienke	Margaret Glowienke
August Glowienke	Margaret Glowienke
Mathilda Glowienke	Margaret Glowienke
Bernard Grenkowitz	Wife, Helen
Mr. and Mrs. Chris Seebacher	Ann and John Kannady
Mr. and Mrs. Nick Funck	Ann and John Kannady
Mr. and Mrs. George Seebacher	Ann and John Kannady
Edward Seebacher	Ann and John Kannady
Maurice J. Kennedy	Mrs. M.J. Kennedy
Raymond J. Neuman	Rose Neuman and Family
Mr. and Mrs. Clarence A. Neuman	Rose Neuman and Family
Ida Gallina	Beverly Ann Battiste
Rev. Edward Reading	Beverly Ann Battiste

IN MEMORIAM

Deceased	Requested by
Torello and Sofia Battiste	Mr. and Mrs. Paul Battiste
Tillie Ghelli	Mr. and Mrs. Paul Battiste
Pietro and Livia Gallina	Mr. and Mrs. Anthony Gallina
John and Rose Slove	Mr. and Mrs. Anthony Gallina
Edward Galuhn	Wife and family
Theresa Biegun	Joseph Biegun
James Ptack	Mrs. Dorothy Ptack
Edward G. Sass	Mary Sass
Mr. and Mrs. Stephen Zokoych	Mary Sass
Frank Zokoych	Mary Sass
William Zokoych	Mary Sass
Deceased of William Boss Family	Mr. and Mrs. William Bargi
Anna Trenker	Mr. and Mrs. Paul Scharneck
Deceased of Marti Family	Family
Gustave Hitzschke	Wife, Patricia
Emilia and Joseph Pruzinec	Daughter, Mary Schwartz
Elizabeth Zigmond	Sister, Mary Schwartz
Frank Schwartz	Wife, Mary Schwartz
William Barlock	Wife, Catherine Barlock
Louis J. Ewald	Wife, Alice Ewald
Dr. Donald G. Ewald	Mother, Alice Ewald
Gustave Hitzschke	Daughter, Nancy
Mr. and Mrs. Tony Mattoracci	Carmella Ingargiola
Alex Reginetz	Carmella Ingargiola

IN MEMORIAM

Deceased	Requested by
Missey Anthony	Mr. and Mrs. Tony Anthony
Mr. and Mrs. Joseph Hebel	Mr. and Mrs. Carl Wirtz
Anton Wirtz	Mr. and Mrs. Carl Wirtz
Mrs. Magdalena Wirtz	Mr. and Mrs. Carl Wirtz
Mrs. Maria Wirtz	Mr. and Mrs. Carl Wirtz
Gustave Hitzschke	Daughter, Barbara
Chris and Marion Schmidt	Chris and Rosalie Schmidt
Phillip Markiewicz	Chris and Rosalie Schmidt
John L. Anselmini	Wife, Ann
Margaret and Wynard Christenson	Bernita, Beverly and Carl
Helen Stubenrauch	Ray Stubenrauch
Otto and Mary Stubenrauch	Ray Stubenrauch
Gilbert and James Fuenfle	Betty Fuenfle
Lenihan and Glzynski Family	L. Lenihan
John J. Sullivan Family	Daughters

YOUR HEART SHALL REJOICE
AND YOUR JOY NO ONE
SHALL TAKE FROM YOU

ST. BONAVENTURE INDEX

A

1912 Olympics, 26
33 East Wacker Drive, 20
50/50 Club, 55, 74
Abbott, Kathryn, 96
Abbott, Virginia, 28
Acquinas, Thomas, 27
Adamowski, Tony, 70
Adams, Al, 61
Adelbert, Sister, 30
Agatha, Sister, 30
Agnes, Sister, 31
Agnesetta, Sister, 31
Agony in the Garden, 95
Aguirre, Haidee, 75, 79
Aguirre, Inelisse, 75, 79
Ahern, Katherine, 69
Alberta, Sister, 30
Alfred, Sister, 30
All Saints Church, 33
Alms, Sister, 30
Altar and Rosary Society, 37, 46, 93
Altgeld Avenue, 19, 25, 38
Alvares, Jose, 69, 79
Amateur Hour, 46
Ambrose, Sister, 30
America, 21
American League, 26
American Revolution, 18
Amidei, Emidio, 41
Anders, C., 41
Anderson, George F., 41
Andreozzi, Gabriel, 41
Angela, Sister, 30
Anglemire, Earl M., 41
Anita Jeanne, Sr. (Mary Frejancz), 39
Anita Therese, Sister, 31
Annamarie, Sister, 31
Anselmini, Philip "Deedy", 41
Antonia, Sister, 30
Aquinas Discussion Club, 46
Aquinas, Sister, 30
Aquinata, Sister, 30
Archambault, Bennett, 24
Arizona, 26
Arok, 72
Ash Manor, 25, 62
Ashland Avenue, 19, 23, 25, 26, 28
Asia, 18, 47
Augustine, Sister, 30
Austin, Sister, 30

B

Bagnorea, Italy, 27
Bahr, George, 41
Balash, Julius, 41
Baleb, L., 26
Balicki, Theodore R., 41
Balon, William E., 41
Bandu, John E., 41
Barajas, Amado, 70
Baranowski, Robert, 61
Bargi, Bernatette, 47
Bargi, Daniel, 68
Bargi, Dolly, 60
Bargi, Karen, 66
Bargi, Kathy, 63
Bargi, Louis, 46
Bargi, Mario, 41, 47
Bargi, Mary, 77
Bargi, Pat, 60, 79, 100

Bargi, Rick, 63
Bargi, Tom, 63
Bargi, Willie, 38, 46
Barlock, Bill, 55
Barnum, Paul T., 41
Barrientos, James, 79
Barsi, Frank, 41
Bartolomei, Egitina, 77
Barts, Clarence, 41
Barts, Gerald, 41
Barts, Lawrence, 41, 74
Barts, William, 41
Baschiere, Ann, 77
Baschiere, Doug, 74, 77
Baske, Henry, 41
Bassick-Alemite Corporation, 24
Battiste, Anna, 77
Battiste, Beverly, 39, 71, 77, 79
Battiste, Paul, 29, 68
Battiste, Tillie, 29
Beavers, Max, 41
Beckenese, Diederick, 22
Beckenese, Louisa, 22, 23
Bedard, Dell, 37, 38
Bedard, Iven, 41
Beeftink, Henry, 41, 45
Begnuche, Frances, 77
Beidron, Raplh, 41
Beitzel, Raymond J., 41
Belvedere, Alois, 41
Benedicta, Sister, 31
Berchmans, Sister, 30
Bernacchi, Elaine, 52
Bernadetta, Sister, 31
Bernardin, Joseph Cardinal, 5, 6, 67
Bernice, Sister, 30
Berrios, Aidy, 75, 79
Berrios, Manuel, 75, 78, 79
Bertolani, Raymond, 41
Bertoncini, Lina, 77
Best, Kenneth, 41
Bettini, Geno, 41
Biagi, Nelda, 77
Bialk, Frank, 22
Bianchi, Frank, 68, 70
Bianchi, Lina, 68, 70
Bickel, Thomas, 63, 75
Biedron, Cynthia R., 41
Biedron, Ralph, 41
Bienias, Josephine, 77
Bieschke, Joseph, 41
Biggins, Thomas, 96
Bingo, 63, 64, 74
Bittner, Larry, 72
Bjurstrom, Pamela Sister, 31
Black Hawk War, 18
Blackstone Hotel, 20
Blaul, Frank, 32
Blaul, Mamie, 29
Boden, James, 41
Boehm, Michael J., 66, 67, 68
Boes, Mary Ann Sister, 31, 59, 79
Boesen, Herbert, 62
Bogacki, Leonard F., 41
Boloe, Walter, 41
Bonaventure, Sister (Kathleen Hill), 31, 39, 50, 100
Boni, Emilia, 77
Bonke, Herbert, 41
Bonke, Leonard, 41
Book of Sentences, 27
Borchardt, Harold, 38, 41
Borchardt, Patricia Sister, 31
Borowski, Walter, 41, 45, 93
Boy Scouts, 47, 55, 79
Boyk, Edmund T., 41

Boyk, Joseph, 41
Boyk, Lawrence, 41
Boyle, Eugene, 41
Boyle, Joseph, 41
Braband, Leonard, 37
Braeckman, George E., 41
Brandey, Norman, 41
Brankey, Edward, 41
Brankey, Raymond, 41
Brendan, Sister, 30
Brennecje, Marilyn, 38
British, 18
Brocato, Frank, 41
Brociek, Florence, 60, 63
Brociek, Jeff, 59
Brogi, Bruno, 41
Brown, Donald J., 41, 45
Brown, Harold, 41
Brown, Joan, 75
Brown, John, 41
Brown, Majorie, 37
Bruno, Donald, 41
Buck, Francis, 33, 55
Budha, Mary Ann Sister, 31
Burgess, Kenneth W., 41
Burke, Leo, 41
Bush, Bernice, 69
Bush, Steve, 69
Butler, James E., 41

C

Cabrini, Mother, 46
Cahill, Philip, 39, 46
Calabrese, Ann, 77
Camilla, Sister, 30
Campo, Joseph, 41
Cannon, Donna Marie, 50
Cantore, Dom, 63
Canty, Jack, 38
Capini, Victor L., 41
Caramelli, Ted, 41
Carbide and Carbon Building, 20
Cariato, Richard, 41
Carlise, Marie, 61
Carmelita, Sister, 30
Carmody, Caroline (Sr. Veronica), 39, 50, 100
Carmody, Frank P., 41
Carnival Committee, 75
Carnival, 71, 72
Carroll, John, 41
Carton, Joseph, 33
Cassidy, Anna, 23, 25
Castro, Nelly, 79
Castro, Nery, 75, 79
Castro, Rogelio, 75, 79
Castro, Tony, 75
Catherine, Sister, 31
Catholic Bishop of Chicago, 25
Catholic Literature Distributors, 48
Cauwels, Charles, 41
Cauwels, Henry J., 41
Cavanaugh, James, 29
Cedar, Willard, 41
Cemignani, Gabriel C., 41
Cernicky, Julia, 93
Challenger Space Shuttle, 75
Charles Ann, Sister, 30
Charles, Sister, 31
Charlotte Marie, Sister, (Margaret Smith), 31, 39, 100
Chateau Thierry, France, 32
Chekas, Walter C., 41

Chelette, Garry, 66
Chelette, Ursula, 66
Chi-Rho Club, 46
Chiappa, Amelia, 77
Chicago, 18, 20, 21, 22, 24, 25, 46, 64, 65, 67, 75
Chicago Board of Trade, 20
Chicago City Council, 78
Chicago Cubs, 26
Chicago Flexible Shaft Company, 24, 25
Chicago Housing Authority, 33
Chicago Police, 28
Chicago River, 18, 21, 25
Chicago Terra Cotta Company, 19, 20
Chicago Theater, 20
Chicago and Northwestern Railroad, 25
Chicago, Bears, 75
Children of Mary Sodality, 46
Christ the King, 19
Choir, Church, 75
Choir, Spanish, 75
Christ the Good Shepherd, 94
Christiansen, William, 41
Christina, Sister, 30
Cicci, Deno, 41
Cicci, Mario, 41
Ciesinski, Alex B., 41
Ciesinski, Harry J., 41
Ciesinski, Hilory, 41
Ciesinski, Sanders, 41
Cijneros, Manuel, 70
Cincinelli, Daniel, 41
Cintron, 68
Cintron, Jose, 67, 68
Cintron, Lydia, 67, 79
Cintron, Tina, 68
Ciucci, Joseph, 41
Clare, Sister, 30
Clark, William E., 41
Clarke, Thomas Jefferson, 24
Class of 1922, 35
Class of 1924, 35
Class of 1925, 35
Class of 1926, 35
Class of 1927, 35
Class of 1930, 35
Class of 1931, 40
Class of 1939, 40
Clement IV, Pope, 27
Clybourn Avenue, 21, 22, 25
Cobb, Ty, 26
Cody, John P., 59, 63, 66, 67
Coggins, Leo P., 55, 56
Colbert, Bertram, 41
Cole, George, 41
Collazo, Isabel, 75
Colleran, James A., 56, 59, 61
Collette Marie, Sister, 31
Conley, Thomas, 58, 59
Connaughton, Maureen Therese, 50
Connelly, Emmett, 41
Connolly, Robert, 41
Conoboy, Lester J., 41
Conroy, Michael, 49
Constance, Sister, 30
Conway, Edward, 53, 59
Conway, Patrick J., 41
Corbett, Phili, 41
Cordaro, Bob, 59
Cordaro, Tony, 59
Correa, Santiago, 69
Cortopassi, Giorgia, 77
Coughlin, Bill, 63
Coughlin, Tony, 63
Council of Catholic Women, 46, 77, 78
Cousins, William, 41
Crenshaw, Derek, 16, 17, 18, 100
Crespo, Jose, 69
Crus, Christina, 68
Cummings, Linda, 66

Cummings, Robert, 66
Cunningham, John P., 61
Cunningham, Kathie, 77
Cunningham, Laetisia, 50
Cusack, James, 41
Cuzzo, Louis J., 41
Cynova, Warren, 41
Czechorski, Edwin, 38

D

Dalke, Kenneth, 41
Damen Avenue, 25, 26, 33
Damen, Arthur, 33
Daniel, Frank, 28, 63
Daniel, Johanna, 63
Daniel, Robert, 41
Daniel, Sister, 30
Daniels, Janet Sister, 31
Davies, Robert, 59
Davis, Sister, 30
Dawson, Frank, 63, 74, 77, 79
Dawson, Rose, 56, 60
DeBartolo, Frank, 25, 62
DeCantillon, Edward, 41
DeMilio, Anna, 93
DeNeri, Sister, 31
DeZetter, Dan, 34
DeZetter, Vincent, 41
Deeken, Fred A., 41
Deering Works of IHC, 21, 25, 26, 33, 97
Deering, James, 21
Deering, William, 21
Dejesus, Nelly, 75
Del Rio, Ivan, 67
Del Rio, Myrian, 67
Delire, Lucius B., 51, 56, 61, 63, 64, 65, 68, 72, 79, 100
Delke, Cecilia, 55
Delke, Kenneth, 41
Dema, Joseph, 41, 45
Deneen, Charles, 23
Dennis Michael, Sister, 31
Desales, Sister, 30
Detroit Tigers, 26
Dettloff, Frank, 37
DiMatteo, Frank, 68
DiMatteo, Patricia, 68
Ditka, Mike, 71
Diversey Emergency Pantry, 61
Diversey Parkway, 19, 22, 23, 24, 25, 26, 28, 30, 37, 38, 64, 71, 75
Doherty, William, 41
Dolan, Kenneth C., 41
Dolores, Sister, 30
Dolorita, Sister, 31
Dominic, Sister, 30
Domitilla, Sister, 31
Dondalski, John, 41
Donlan, James, 46, 51
Donna Marie, Sister, 31
Dooley, Mike, 79
Dorothy, Sister, 30
Dorsch, Darlene, 74
Dorsey, G. A., 23
Douvris, Andres, 42
Drew, Robert, 37
Duever, Louise, 34
Duffy, Peter, 39, 51
Dunleavy, Catherine, 94
Durand, Lawrence, 42
Duwentester, Helen, 37
Dwyer, George R., 42
Dwyer, Michael, 42
Dwyer, Robert, 42
Dwyer, William A., 42
Dzike, Edward T., 42

E

Easpamer, Frank, 58
Easton, William, 31
Eddy, Kenneth, 42
Edward Alishia, Sister, 31
Edward, Henry, 42
Edward, Sister, 30
Edwardetta, Sister, 31
Ehmann, Albert, 42
Ehrenberg, Nick, 63
Ehrenberg, Norma, 60, 63, 77, 79, 100
Eileen Marie, Sister, 30
Elizabeth, Sister, 30
Ellis Island, 75
Ellman, Werned, 42
Elwart, Dick, 47, 71, 74, 75
Enabling Act, 18
England, 21
Erie Canal, 18
Esposito, Rita Sister, 31
Ethelreda, Sister, 30
Etten, Van, 26
Eucharista, Sister, 30
Europe, 47
Evangelista, Sister, 30
Evans, Herbert O., 42
Evelyn, Sister, 31

F

Faggi, Aurdey, 47
Fahey, Peggy
Faity, Richard C., 42
Fall Festival, 51, 53
Fanelli, Charles, 64
Fannucchi, Jim, 63, 77
Fanucchi, Josephine, 77
Fatima Devotions, 46
Faucher, Eugene, 58, 59, 60
Feliciano, Efrain, 70, 79
Feliciano, Iraida, 70, 79
Felski, Norbert, 42
Fenelli, Deno, 42
Ferguson, Daniel R., 28, 42, 45
Ferjancy, Anita Jeanne, 50
Fester, Leonard, 42
Fidelis, Sister, 30
Field Museum, 23
Filetti, A., 42
Filetti, Michael, 42
Finger, Joseph, 50
Fini, Peter, 42
Fink, Emil, 42
Finley, John, 74
Finnelli, Shirley, 60
Fiore, Martin, 42
Fisher Building, 20
Fitzgerald, Gerald, 95
Fitzmaurice, Danny, 61
Fitzner, Henry, 42
Fitzner, James J., 42
Flanagan, Anna, 93
Fletcher Street, 32
Florita, Sister, 31
Flosi, Nancy, 77
Flugardi, Marvin, 42
Flynn, Joseph P., 42
Foley, Patricia, 71, 75, 100
Foley, Ralph, 75
Forde, James, 42
Formella, Edward, 42
Forssander, John, 42
Forssander, Paul, 42
Fort Dearborn, 18
Forty Hour Devotions, 46
Foster, Rose, 65, 75, 79, 100
Fox Indians, 18

Foy, Joseph, 42
Foy, Martin S., 42, 45
Foy, Vincent E., 42
Foy, W. S., 42
France, 18, 32
Francis Therese, Sister (Lucille Jankoski), 39
Francis Xavier, Sister, 30
Francis, Mary Sister, 30, 93
Franciscan Order, 27
Franke, Ray, 42
Frateschi, Felix, 42
Frateschi, Lawrence, 42
Frederick, Norman, 42
Frederick, Richard, 42
Frederick, Sister, 31
Fredian, Eugene J., 42
Fredian, Therese, 38
Fredora, Joseph W., 42
Freiboth, Ray, 42
Frejancz, Mary (Anita Jeanne, Sister), 39
Friend, Dr. Alex J. G., 25
Fullerton Avenue, 21, 28
Funck, Nicholas, 34, 42

G

Gaba, Joseph J., 42
Gabinski, Theris M., 10, 64, 76, 78
Gabriel, Sister, 30
Gabriel, Walter, 42
Gagliano, Frank T., 42
Gagliano, Joseph, 42
Gagliano, Louis, 42
Galli, Mary, 77
Galuhn, Edward J., 42, 46, 66
Galuhn, Henry, 42
Galuhn, Margaret (Dolly), 46, 60, 66, 67
Gannon, Thomas, 42
Garlin, Edward S., 42
Gatto, Anthony C., 42
Gatto, Dorothy, 71, 75
Gaughan, Anthony, 50, 53
Gaynor, James G., 53
Gdula, Edward, 42, 46
Gdula, Walter, 42
Gemignani, Anthony, 42, 45
Gemignani, Elisa, 77
Genevieve, Sister, 30
Geni, John, 42
Gentili, Leo O., 42
George Agnes, Sister, 31
George Street, 25
Georgeson, Tony, 75, 77
Geraghty, Peter, 28
Gerard, Sister, 30
Gerhos, Charles, 42
Germania Club Building, 20
Gernhofer, Bob, 67
Gernhofer, Margie, 67
Gernhofer, Niki, 67
Gernhofer, Rick, 67
Gerovese, Salvador J., 42
Gertie, Francis H., 42
Gertie, Jacob J., 42
Getz, Joseh, 42
Ghilardi, Premetta, 77
Ghimenti, Joseph, 42
Giannoni, Barbara, 75
Giannotti, Pietro, 77
Gilberta, Sister, 30
Gilboy, Paul, 42
Gilboy, Ralph, 42
Gillis, Clifford, 42
Gillis, Winford, 42
Gilmore-McHugh, Lois, 79
Giltner, Ernest C., 42
Ginnotti, Gina, 77

Girl Scouts, 47, 48, 55, 56
Glauda, Alfred, 42
Glowienke, Leo, 42
Glowienke, William P., 42
Glowienke, Gary, 63
Good Councel, Sister, 31
Good Shepherd, Sister, 30
Gorman, James P., 42
Gorman, John P., 42, 45
Gorman, Joseph, 34, 66
Gorman, Mary, 34
Gorman, Viola, 45, 66, 79
Goss, George, 42
Goss, William, 42
Grace, Sister, 31
Grady, John, 42
Graff, Austin, 100
Graff, Robert, 100
Great Lakes, 17, 18
Greenwood Avenue, 19
Gregory X, Pope, 27
Groth, Gerry, 47
Groth, Walter, 42
Gryewla, George, 42
Guerra, Peter, 42
Gugliotta, Elda, 78, 79
Guidotti, John V., 42
Guttilla, Mary, 61
Guttilla, Nick, 61
Guttilla, Peter, 61

H

Haack, Paul, 42
Habel, Arthur, 42
Halley's Comet, 75, 97
Hannigan, James, 42
Hannigan, John F., 42
Hannigan, Mary Lillian, 42
Hannigan, Richard, 42
Hansen, Michael J., 42
Hart, Frederic J., 42
Hastings, Thomas, 42
Hays, Norman R., 42
Hebel, George, 42
Heim, Michael, 42
Helfrich, George, 55, 59
Hemmer, Virginia, 56
Henrietta, Sister, 31
Hepp, Arthur, 42
Hermitage Avenue, 22, 23
Herr, George, 42
Herr, John J., 42
Herrmann, Richard T., 42
Hert, Edward D., 42
Hert, George J., 42
Hert, James D., 42
Higgins, John W., 42
High School Club, 46
Hilary, Sister, 31
Hill, Genevieve, 71
Hill, Edmund B., 42
Hill, John P., 42
Hill, Joseph E., 29, 42
Hill, Joseph, 54
Hill, Kathleen (Sr. Bonaventure), 31, 39, 50, 100
Hill, Kevin, 42, 53
Hill, Margaret, 29
Hillinger, Raymond P., 55
Hilsher, Lorretta, 47
Hilsher, Margaret, 49
Hitterman, Art, 74, 75
Hoehne, Barbara, 60
Hogan, Joan, 79
Hollis, Frank, 42
Holy Cross Fathers, 62
Holy Hill, 78

Holy Name Cathedral, 56
Holy Name Society, 46, 61
Holy Name Society, Junior, 46
Hopp, Kenneth, 38
Hopper, Roger, 59
Horner, William E., 42
Hubeck, Steve Mr. and Mrs., 57
Hubeck, Steve, 60
Hubeck, Trudy, 60
Huber, Irving, 42
Huck, John W., 42
Huslein, Margaret, 93

I

Ignatius, Sister, 31
Illini Indians, 18
Illinois Brick Company, 25
Illinois Racing Commission, 25
Illinois Territory, 18
Illinois, 18
Image of Sacred Heart of Jesus, 96
Immacula Pace, Sister, 50
Immaculate Conception Sodality, 46
Immaculate Heart of Mary, 96
Ims, Sister, 30
Inda, Richard, 42
Inquiry Classes for Non-Catholics, 46
International Harvester Company, 21, 33, 97
Ireland, 28
Irene, Sister, 31
Irma Joseph, Sister, 31
Italian Catholic Federation, 61, 64, 77
Iven, Robert, 42

J

Jackicic, Sharon, 50
Jackson, Bill, 41
Jackson, Mildred, 50, 100
Jacobs, Christopher, 50
Jakick, Tom, 42
Jakob, Henry, 42
Jakubiec, Henry C., 42
James, Anthony, 42
Jancovic, Edward S., 42
Jane Frances, Sister, 30
Jane Margaret, Sister, 31
Jankoski, Clarence, 42
Jankoski, Eugene, 42
Jankoski, Lawrence, 42
Jankoski, Lucille (Francis Therese, Sister), 39, 50
Jankowski, Art, 42
Jankowski, Frances Therese, 50
Janowitz, Joseph, 42
Jarlath, Sister, 31
Jay, Edward Jr., 42
Jeanette, Sister, 31
Jennings, Eugene, 42
Jennings, James T., 42
Jerome, Sister, 31
Jett, John, 42
Joan Marie, Sister, 30
Joanne, Sister, 30
Joel, Sister, 31
John Edwin, Sister, 31
John XXIII, Pope, 56
John-Paul I, Pope, 65
John-Paul II, Pope, 4, 65
Johnson, Francine, 79
Johnson, Minnie, 61
Joliet Diocese, 50
Joliet Prison, 23
Joliet, Louis, 18
Joseph, Sister, 31

Jubilee Year, 75, 78
Jungers, Charles, 42
Jurgenson, Robert, 42, 45

K

Kackert, Bernard, 42, 74
Kahles, Nick, 42
Kahles, Peter, 42
Kair, Franklin J., 42
Kanka, Raymond, 42
Kapuscinski, Watler, 42
Karl, Frank W., 42
Karl, George, 42
Karl, Gerry, 47
Karl, Kathy, 62
Karl, Walter, 42
Karlinski, Marilyn Sister, 31
Kasper, Fran, 57
Kasper, George, 77
Kass, Benjamin, 42
Kathleen Edward, Sister, 31
Kawka, Raymond, 42
Kazik, Lydia, 48
Kazik, Norbert, 48
Kazovich, Joseph, 42
Keil, George W., 42
Kelleher, Mickey, 72
Keller, Jack, 42
Keller, William, 42
Kelly, John, 61
Kelly, John Rev., 42, 46, 47, 48, 55
Kelly, Martin, 42
Kelly, Patrick, 75
Kelly, Richard, 42
Kelly, Robert, 43
Kelly, Thomas, 43
Kennedy, Colleen, 79
Kennedy, James, 43
Kennedy, John F., 53
Kennedy, Maurice J., 43
Kennedy, Robert F., 53
Kenneth, Sister, 31
Kevin, Sister, 31
Kilcullen, Bob, 71
Kilduff, Bill, 43
Kilduff, Tom, 43
Kilgallan, Sean, 54
King, Coleman M., 43
King, Donna, 49
King, Ernest, 18, 100
King, James M., 43
King, Margaret (Thomas Agnes, Sister), 39, 50
King, Martin Luther, 53
Kirschbaum, Dennis A., 54
Kirschbaum, Doloris, 1, 79
Kirschbaum, Marie, 61, 79, 100
Kirschbaum, Paul, 61, 74
Kirschbaum, Rita, 61
Klein, J., 43
Klein, Robert J., 43
Klein, William, 43
Kloss, Ann, 38
Kloss, Joseph P, Jr., 43
Klost, Joseph, 43
Klostermann, Ignatius, 43
Klostermann, John, 43
Knight, Elaine, 58
Knight, Jessie, 52
Knights and Handmaids of the Blessed Sacrament
Knowlson, James S., 24
Koeneke, R. J., 43
Kollar, George, 31
Kolle, John, 43
Korean War, 24, 49
Koster, Vistor, 93

Koutouzou, Tina, 48
Kowalski, Eleanor, 77
Kowar, Luann, 75
Kozio, Ted, 64
Krauser, Albert, 79, 100
Krerowicz, John, 43
Krzykowski, Richard, 43
Kubat, Dolores, 77
Kuerbs, Clement, 43
Kuester, Augusta, 19
Kulanda, Jeannette, 77
Kulas, Leroy, 43
Kulis, Chet, 65
Kunstadt, Ernest, 43
Kuntz, Paul J., 43
Kunz, Fred J., 43
Kunz, John, 43
Kunz, Richard, 75
Kunz, Tony, 43
Kusnicki, George, 43
Kusnicki, Joseph, 43

L

LaGrange, Illinois 20, 38, 68
LaPaglia, Angelo, 64
LaSalle Photo, 100
LaSalle, 18
Lackowski, John A., 43
Lackowski, Sohpie, 60
Ladda, Louis, 43
Lake View, 18, 19, 26
Lakowski, Edward A., 43
Lakowski, Robert, 43
Lamberti, Esmerald, 77
Landini, Elmer, 20
Landini, Eveo, 43
Landini, Giuseppe, 77
Landini, Jeanne, 39
Landini, Joseph I., 43
Landini, Renato, 43
Landini, Roland, 43
Landini, Rose, 52
Lange, George J., 43
Langluine, Edward J., 43
Lapinski, Jerry, 71
Lathrop, Homes Julia, 21, 25, 33, 61
Laura Annette, Sister, 30
Lawrence James, Sister, 30
Laxner, Edwin, 43
LePuy, France, 30
Leavitt Street, 21
Leavitt Street, 21
Lebron, Bernarda, 78
Lebron, Maxinino, 78
Lechessi, Helen, 47
Lechman, Adam J., 43
Lectors & Commentators, 64, 77
Legion of Decency, 46
Legion of Mary, 78
Lehman, Joseph, 43
Lemberg, Edward, 43
Lenzi, Aldo, 43
Leonard, Sister, 31
Leonard, William, 38
Levitzke, George A., 43
Lewandowski, John, 43
Lichter, Andrew, 43
Lietz, Jack T., 43
Lietz, T. W., 93
Liguori, Sister, 30, 69
Lincoln Street, 25
Lindmeier, Adele, 77
Lindmeier, Stanley, 43, 58, 74
Linus, Sister, 30
Liturgy Committee, 64
Litz, Herbert R., 43
Litz, John R., 43

Lombard, Peter, 27
Long, William P., 33, 36, 51, 71
Loring, Sandford, 19
Loyola University, 33
Loyola, Sister, 30
Lubner, Paul P., 43
Luby, William V., 43
Lucas, H. J., 19
Lucca Italy, 47, 69
Luetgert, A. L. Sausage Works, 22, 25
Luetgert, Adolph Louis, 22, 23
Lusak, John, 43
Luthi, Bill, 43
Lynak, Rosalien, 50
Lynch, Dolores Sister, 31
Lynch, John W., 43
Lynch, Norman W., 43
Lynch, Rosalien, 50
Lyons, Eugene F., 39, 50, 55
Lyons, France, 27

M

Mackey, Edward, 43
Madeline, Sister, 30
Maggie, Patty, 56
Magnanenzi, Fred, 43
Magnanenzi, John, 43
Maher, Robert J., 43
Majewski, Tom, 43
Makurat, Joseph, 37, 43
Malcolm X, 53
Malcolm, Lawrence, 61, 62, 63, 64
Malczewski, Chester J., 54
Maldonado, Bernadina, 78, 79
Maldonado, ElPedio, 78, 79
Mallable Iron, 25
Maloney, Tom, 74
Mancuso, Joseph, 43
Mancuso, Peter, 43
Manfredi, Ralph, 43
Mangiameli, Anthony, 43
Mangiameli, S. A., 43
Mangiameli, Vincent, 43
Manhattan Building, 20
Maninfior, Laura, 77
Mannina, Sam, 43
Marach, Norbert, 43
Marcella, Sister, 31
Marcheschi, Rina, 77
Marchetti, Lola, 77
Marchini, Albert, 36, 57, 74
Marchini, Ersilia, 59
Marchini, Jeannie, 59
Marchini, Kenneth, 59
Marchini, Laida, 36, 57, 77, 79
Marchini, Orland, 43
Marchini, Paolo, 59
Marczyk, Therese Sister, 31
Maree, John, 43
Margaret Flaherty, Sister, 31
Margaret M., Sister, 30
Margaret, Sister, 31
Marguerite, Sister, 31
Mariana Avenue, 25
Marie Clarice, Sister, 31
Mariettina, Sister, 31
Marion Award, 56
Mark, Sister, 31
Marquette, Fr., 18
Marshfield Avenue, 23, 25, 37, 38
Marszalek, Edward J., 43
Marszalek, Frank P., 43
Marszalek, Joseph, 43
Martin, Sister, 31
Martinez, Charles, 58
Martinez, E., 3
Martorano, Jack, 43

Martorano, Mary, 47
Mary and Joseph Circle, 47, 61
Match Game, 63
Matrango, Victor, 43
Matteucci, Licena, 77
Maureen Francis, Sister, 31
Maurita, Sister, 31
Maxwell, William J., 43
May, Roy, 43
Maziarka, Ron, 77
McClem, Pat, 47
McCormick Harvester Company, 21
McCormick, Cyrus Hall, 21
McCulloch, Charles I., 43
McDermott, Bill, 63
McDermott, James, 62
McDermott, Marybeth, 50
McDermott, Sarah, 47
McDonough, Bernard, 43
McDonough, Eugene, 43, 53
McDonough, John J., 43
McDonough, Mr. and Mrs., 93
McDonough, Thomas, 43
McElboy, Jerome J., 43
McEvilly, John, 43
McEvilly, Thomas, 43
McFarland, John, 43, 45
McGrath, Francis, 50, 56, 51, 71
McGuigan, John, 43
McGuigan, Joseph, 43
McGuire, Martin J., 28, 33, 96
McHugh, Mary, 37
McIntyre, John, 43
McIntyre, Thomas A., 43
McKay, Russell, 43
McKeekin, Betty, 63
McKenna, Mary, 29
McKeown, Mary, 95
Mei, Ann, 67, 77
Mei, Nick, 67
Mellenthin, Charlotte, 58
Mendez, Angelo, 79
Mendez, Carmen, 79
Menkol, S., 43
Mercedes, Sister, 31
Merchandise Mart, 20
Mertes, Frank, 43
Metcalf, Roy, 77, 79
Meyer, Albert G., 49, 50, 71
Meyer, Gloria, 52, 60, 79, 100
Meyer, Nick, 52
Meyer, William, 43
Michael Ann, Sister, 30
Michael, Sister, 31
Mignano, Joe, 43
Mignano, Victor, 43
Milanowski, Florian, 43
Mildred, Jackson Sister, 31, 100
Milkovich, Robert, 43
Miller, Dorothy, 57
Miller, Ed, 41
Miller, Marvin, 57
Miller, Wanda, 78, 79
Minkalis, Charles, 43
Miriam Therese, Sister, 30
Mischke, Richard W., 43
Mitzlaff, Herbert J., 43
Modesta, Sister, 31
Mollitor, Joseph, 26
Monahan, Tecla, 77, 79
Monica, Sister, 31
Moran, Thomas A., 64
Moran, Vincent J., 36, 37, 38, 41, 49, 50, 51, 52, 55, 72
Moreau House, 62
Morgan, Joseph A., 43
Morin, Joseph J., 60
Morris, Johnny, 71
Moscinski, Daniel H., 43
Motsch, Mary, 47, 48, 71, 74

Mound Builders, 18
Mount, Henry, 43
Moysis, Stephen R., 43, 45
Mullen, John J., 43
Muller, Louis, 94
Murphy, George E., 43
Murray, Michael J., 2, 4, 65, 67, 77, 79, 100
Murray, Michael J., 51
Musial, Diane Sister, 31, 62
Muza, Fred, 43
Myskow, Christine Sister, 31, 59

N

Nadolny, Louis, 43
Najjar, Charles, 43
Najjar, Leonard, 43
National League, 26
Naumann, Lenny, 59
Needham, John, 43
Nelson, James, 43
Neri, Dennis, 68
Neri, Geno, 43, 48
Neri, Marie, 48
Neri, Martha, 68
Nettnier, Fred, 43
Netzel, Charles G., 43
Netzel, Jeannie, 50
Netzel, Kenneth, 43
Neuman, Charles, 43
Nevins, Donald, 75
New Mexico, 26
News and Views, 41, 45
Nicholas, Sister, 30
Niegar, John T., 43
Nimietz, Bobby, 38
Nitsch, Alvin W., 43
Nora, Sister, 31
Norbert, Sister, 30
Norine, Sister, 31
North America, 17
North American Indians, 18
North Atlantic, 26, 75
Northwest Territory, 18
Northwestern Terra Cotta Works, 19, 20, 26, 38
Norton, John W., 43
Norton, Kenneth, 43
Novelli, Mario, 43

O

O'Brien, Eileen, 79
O'Callaghan, Joseph, 33
O'Connor, Daniel, 43
O'Connor, Ed, 75
O'Connor, James, 43
O'Connor, Margaret, 29
O'Connor, Mary Ellen (Ryan), 29
O'Connor, William, 43
O'Donnell, Thomas V., 43
O'Grady, John P., 43
O'Ken, Robert P., 43
O'Leary, Cornelius, 43
O'Malley, Patrick, 43
O'Shana, Robert, 43, 45
Obee, Kurt, 43
Oberman, Martin J., 14
Off, William, 43
Ohio, 19
Ojibwa Indians, 18
Old Capital Building, 20
Olea, Pedro, 69
Oleszizuk, Steve, 62
Olijar, John N., 43
Olinski, Bernard, 43

Oliver, Sister, 30
Ori, Eleanor, 70
Osceike, Josephine, 78, 79
Ostrowski, Matthew, 49
Ott, Bill, 43
Ott, George A., 43
Ott, William, 43
Ottawa, Indiana, 18
Our Lady of Sorrows, 94

P

Pacini, Mara, 77
Pagnucci, Armando, 43
Palluck, Joseph, 47, 93
Palluck, Pat, 47
Paluch, Joe, 41
Paoli, Alfred, 43
Paoli, Attilio, 43
Paoli, Ben, 43
Paoli, Lea, 77
Paoli, Mark, 63
Paoli, Mary, 60
Paoli, Ted, 63
Paolini, Edward, 43
Paolini, Joseph, 43
Papucci, Aldo, 43
Papucci, Ernie, 66
Papucci, Settima, 77
Papucci, Val, 74
Pardini, Eno, 43
Parenti, Nella, 77
Parish Council, 59
Parish Library, 46
Parker, Eugene, 58, 59, 60, 62
Parker, Margaret Sister, 31
Parkes, Sylvia Sister, 31
Paschke, George N., 44
Pasquinelli, Alfred, 46
Pasquinelli, Josephine, 46
Patock, Arnold, 44
Patock, Edward, 44
Patock, Lawrence, 44
Patock, Norbert, 44, 45
Patock, Ralph, 44
Patrick Marie, Sister, 31
Pattock, Clarence J., 44
Pattullo, Cathy, 69
Pattullo, Tom, 69
Paul VI, Pope, 65
Paula, Sister, 31
Paulina Street Association, 38
Paulina Street, 25, 26, 38, 56, 64, 71
Pauline, Sister, 31
Paylor, Edward, 44
Pecson, Andy, 75, 77, 79, 100
Pecson, Nestor, 100
Peel, Sir Robert, 28
Pekara, Sue, 64
Pekara, Tom, 64
Pellegrini, Alvin, 48
Pellegrini, Corinne, 48
Pellegrini, Josephine, 75
Pellegrini, Lorraine, 46
Pellegrini, Salvio, 47
Pellicore, Edward, 36
Pellicore, George, 29
Pellicore, Susan, 29
Pellus, William, 44
Penz, Herman, 44
Perez, Luey, 79
Peron, Joseph, 44
Perpetua, Sister, 31
Perr, Ray, 44
Peskuent, George, 44
Peters, William, 44
Peterson, Candy, 64
Peterson, Ernie, 64

Peterson, Gerry, 77, 79
Peterson, John, 64
Petrinec, John, 44
Petronilla, Sister, 30, 50
Phelan, Joseph, 33
Philomene, Sister, 30
Pia, Leo, 44
Piagentini, Angelo, 44
Pierazzi, Mariza, 77
Pierre, Sister, 31
Pierucci, Angelo, 79
Pierucci, Imola, 77
Pionke, Leo, 44
Pius XII, Pope, 37, 47, 69
Pizzi, Angelo, 44
Poland, 65
Polinski, Frank, 44
Polinski, Leonard J., 44
Pollack, H., 44
Pollack, John J., 44
Poltrock, Charles, 74
Pompa, Roger, 59
Poppenga, Edward, 44, 46
Poppenga, Emily, 46
Pottawattomie Indians, 18
Prato, Ann, 58
Prato, Gary, 63
Prato, Harry, 74
Prato, Henry, 44
Prato, Nestor, 44
Prayer Group, 79
Pre-Cana Conference, 46
Priami, Al, 61, 74
Priami, Irene, 77, 79
Prichard, Mrs., 94
Przyleyski, Elaine, 47
Ptack, Dorothy, 48, 71
Ptack, James, 37, 38, 44, 48
Ptack, Jeannette, 52
Puccinelli, George, 44, 64, 93

Q

Quigley Seminary, 39, 59
Quinn, Peter, 28

R

Radtke, Thomas S., 44
Ragus, James J., 44
Railway Exchange Building, 20
Rambert, Harold, 44
Rambert, Hattie, 93
Ranachowski, Leo, 74
Ranachowski, Maryann, 56
Randazzo, Thomas, 44
Raschke, Harold, 44
Ratti, Olga, 77
Raymond, Sister, 30
Reading, Fr., 49, 50
Reagan, Ronald, 7, 75
Reddel, Raymond, 44
Redini, Andy, 44
Reebie Storage Building, 20
Reedy, Mary, 34
Regina, Sister, 30
Rehberger, Arthur, 44
Reiche, Arthur W., 44
Reimer, Louis, 19
Reimer-Kuester Brick Manufacturing Co., 19, 28
Reinert, William J., 44
Reiss, John, 44
Reitmeier, John J., 44
Reliance Building, 20
Rene, Sister, 31
Renkert, Frank, 77

Repp, John, 44
Repp, Matthew, 44
Repp, Thomas, 44
Resko, Martin, 44
Reynolds, Margaret Sister, 31
Rhode, Bishop, 28
Rialto Theater, 20
Riccomini, Dario, 44
Ridolfi, Adolph, 38, 44
Ridolfi, Rose, 77
Riley, Peter, 47, 49
Riley, Thomas A., 44
Rimar, Rosemary, 79
Robert Marie, Sister, 31
Roberta, Sister, 30, 39
Roberts, Walter, 44
Robey Street, 25, 33
Rodriguez, Ester, 78, 79
Rodriguez, Lorenzo, 78, 79
Roeder, Chris, 44
Roeder, Nick, 62
Roeder, Richard E., 44
Rogers, James J., 44
Rohde, George, 44
Roman, Dennis W., 44
Roman, Felicita, 67, 70, 78, 79
Roman, Sister, 31
Roman, Tito, 67, 70, 78, 79
Romanowski, Clarence W., 44
Ronald, Sister, 31
Rondoni, Eugene, 44
Rookery Building, 20
Rosalie Carmel, Sister, 31
Rosaria, Sister, 31
Rosch, Marguerite, 38, 69
Rosch, Nicholas, 38, 69
Roscop, Lorretta, 47
Rose, Sister, 31
Rosenberg, Alderman, 56
Rostenkowski, Dan, 9
Ruben, Gomez, 63
Russo, Sam, 44
Ruta, Sharon, 68
Ruth, Sister, 31
Ryan, Dennis S., 26, 29, 47, 50, 95
Ryan, James J., 44
Ryan, John, 32
Ryan, Mary Ellen (O'Connor), 29, 50, 95
Ryan, T. J., 44
Ryan, Willian D., 41, 44, 50, 69

S

Sac Indians, 18
Sacred Heart Devotions, 46
Sacred Heart League, 46
Sacred Heart, 30
Sacred Theology, 27
Saint Ann, 93
Saint Barbara, 94
Saint Bonaventure, 27, 63, 94, 97, 98, 99
Saint Francis of Assisi, 95, 97
Saint Gemma Galgani, 64, 68, 69, 70
Saint Mary Magdalene, 94
Saint Patrick, 93
Saint Thomas Aquinas, 95
Saisi, Albert, 44
Salems, Earl H., 44
Samuel, Sister, 31
Santiago, Elvira, 79
Santoni, Aldo, 44
Santoni, Angelo, 44
Santos, Antero, 69, 79
Santos, John, 63
Sasokovich, Stephen, 44
Schaefer, Ellard F., 44
Scharneck, Gladys, 77
Schell, Antone, 44

Schemrowski, George, 44
Schifo, Francis F., 44
Schifo, Louis S., 44
Schlake, William E., 25
Schlapinski, Bernice, 46, 60, 77, 79
Schlapinski, Ken, 63
Schlapinski, Raymond, 46
Schmidt, Nick, 44
Schmidt, Tom, 44
Schneider School, 26
Schoenberg, Otto, 38
Scholtes, Butch, 59
Schroeder, Irvin, 44
Schulte, Frank, 26
Schultz, George, 44
Scuderi, Baldassare J., 44
Scuderi, Mary, 75
Sebastian, Sister, 31
Seebacher, Edward, 47
Seebacher, Ester, 34
Seebacher, George, 28, 34, 44, 71
Seebacher, Sue, 34
Seng, Daniel, 79
Seno, Frederick A., 44
Settipane, Sal, 57
Shamroski, George, 44
Shanahan, Dennis J., 44
Shanahan, Lawrence, 44
Shanannan, Geraldine Sister, 31
Sheiffield Avenue Police Station, 22
Sheridan, Fr., 49
Siedlecki, Edmond, 78
Silorski, Edward, 44
Simon, Paul, 11
Simon, Richard T., 68, 77, 79
Sinkovich, Edward, 44
Sirotzke, James, 44
Sisi, Adam, 59
Sisters of St. Joseph, 15, 30, 38, 59, 62
Sixtus IV, Pope, 27
Sixtus V, Pope, 27
Skibicki, Chester A., 49
Skibicki, Daria, 48
Skibicki, Raymond, 44
Skibicki, Richard, 44, 48
Skibicki, Victor, 44
Slakis, Albert J., 44
Smith, C. B., 24
Smith, Jack, 44
Smith, James C., 26
Smith, John Jr., 44
Smith, Margaret, (Sr. Charlotte Marie), 34, 39, 50, 100
Smullen, J. P., 44
Snedeker, C. Mrs., 44
Snedeker, Charles, 44
Sobchak, Leroy R., 44
Soldier's Field, 38
Soldier's Field, 46
Soldwisch, Robert, 44
Solin, Joseph, 44
Solt, Lambert A., 44
South America, 17
Souvigny, Edward N., 44
Spadafora, Michael, 44, 45
Spinabella, Albert, 44
Spionabella, Rigoletto, 44
Springfield, Illinois, 20
St. Aloysius Parish, 62
St. Alphonsus Church, 26
St. Ambrose Parish, 64
St. Andrews Church, 26
St. Bonaventure Church, 15, 19, 23, 25, 26, 29, 30, 31, 32, 33, 36, 39, 41, 45, 46, 47, 49, 50, 51, 55, 56, 58, 59, 61, 64, 67, 68, 71, 75, 78, 97
St. Bonaventure Convent, 28, 33, 37, 38, 39, 47
St. Bonaventure Field, 37
St. Bonaventure Widgets, 56

St. Bonaventure's School, 36, 51, 59, 62
St. Francis of Assisi, 27
St. Francis of Rome Parish, 56
St. John Vianney Church, 64
St. Joseph and Ann Parish, 62
St. Josephat Church, 26
St. Louis, Missouri, 28
St. Mary of the Lake Parish, 67
St. Philip Neri Church, 55
St. Raymond de Penafort Church, 56
St. Theresa of Palatine, 64
St. Thomas Apostle School, 20
St. Thomas Aquinas Church, 36
St. Vincent Depaul, 26
St. Xavier School, 68
Stahl, James, 44, 93
Stanhibel, Ken, 79
Stanislaus, Sister, 31
Stanton, Peter, 93
Stasica, Corrine, 75
Stasica, Robert, 48
Stations of the Cross, 93
Statue of Liberty, 75, 97
Steiner, Ed, 47, 52, 63, 77
Steiner, John, 100
Stella, Sister, 30
Stempien, Edmund, 44
Stephen, Rev., 62
Stewart & Clark Manufacturing Company, 24
Stewart, John K., 24
Stewart-Warner Corporation, 24, 25, 26, 97
Stewart-Warner Speedometer Corporation, 24
Stoll, Al, 47
Stopa, Ray, 77, 79
Stopa, Robert, 47
Stopa, Roberta, 47
Stritch, Samual, 38, 39
Strmiska, Albert, 44
Stubenrauch, Kathy, 75, 77, 79
Stubenrauch, Peggy, 65
Stubenrauch, Raymond, 34
Stubenrauch, Viola, 34
Sullivan Girls, 29
Sulzer, Donald, 44
Szfranski, Frank, 44
Szfranski, Henry, 44
Szfranski, Leroy, 44
Szmkowski, Edmund, 44
Szymczak, Irene, 60
Szymkowski, Edward J., 44

T

Taft, William Howard, 26
Tappings, Tom, 75
Tarnowski, Harry, 44
Taylor, Donald, 44
Taylor, Ed., 44
Taylor, George, 44
Tenner, Walter J., 44
Tepich, Rod, 44
Terra Cotta Place
Tessner, Elmer, 44
Theis, Anthony J., 44
Theodore, Conrad, 37

Tholke, Edward T., 44
Thomas Agnes, Sister, (Margaret King), 31, 39
Thompson, James R., 8
Thompson, Peter J., 44
Thomson, Ellsworth E., 44
Thorpe, Jim, 26
Tinucci, George, 44
Titanic, 26, 75
Tobin, Frank, 74
Topka, Matthew, 44
Torgersen, Sue Sister, 31
Tossi, Francis J., 44
Touhey, William J., 44
Tramutola, John, 63
Treaty of Paris, 18
Tree Studio, 20
Trocke, Charles G., 44
Troescher Building, 20
Tumele, Michael, 44
Turco, Hary, 44
Tutankhamen, 20

U

Udrow, Leroy, 44
Udrow, William, 44
Ugel, Chuck, 52
Uller, Clinton, 26, 94
United States, 18, 20, 26, 28, 32, 39, 64
University of Paris, 27
Uramkin, Michael J., 44
Ursula, Sister, 31
Uzdrowski, Wilbur F., 44

V

Valdez, Joan, 79
Valeria, Sister, 31
Van Etten, Mr., 26
Vatican II, 53, 58, 59
Venice Hall, 78
Vernon, George, 44
Vernon, Robert, 44
Veronica, Sister, (Caroline Carmody), 31, 39, 100
Vietnam, 53, 54
Vincent, Alice Sister, 31
Virgina, Sister, 30
Volk, John, 44
Von Buxtaele, J., 44

W

Waeh, Don, 58
Wagner, Herb, 44
Wagner, Joseph, 44
Wagner, Peter J., 44
Walsh, Anthony A., 44, 45
Ward, Cornelius, 93
Ward, Hannah, 93
Ward, John, 96
Ward, Mr. & Mrs. C. J., 93
Ward, Rosemry, 47
Ward, Tarcisius, 50
Ward, Thomas, 96

Warner Instrument Company, 24
Warner, Edwin B., 44
Washington, Harold, 13, 76
Weber, Charlie, 38
Weber, Henry, 28
Webster Avenue, 22
Weglarz, Stan, 44
Wehrheim, Jeanne, 77
Weindorfer, Don, 59
Weindorfer, Emilia, 59
Weiser, Francis W., 44
Welker, Lorraine Sister, 31
Wellington Avenue, 26
Wengler, Thomas, 44
Wenholz, Henry M., 44
Wenserski, Daniel, 44
Werner, Robert, 44
Whelan, Jack, 29
Wiedlin, George, 44
Wiegert, Raymond, 38
Wilcox, Thomas, 44
Wilhelm, A. J., 44
Wilks, Pearl, 47
Willer, Edward, 44
Williams, George, 45
Williams, John, 45
Willis, Henry, 26
Wilma, Sister, 30
Winitred, Mrs., 93
Winnebago Indians, 18
Wirtz, Carl, 74
Witt, Charles, 45
Witt, Wally, 63
Witt, William, 45
Wojciechowski, Leroy, 38
Wojcieckowski, G., 45
Wojtezak, Eugene S., 45
Wolcott, 25
Wolf, Corinne, 34
Wolf, John, 45
Wolf, William, 45
Wolfram, 22, 25
Wolniewicz, John, 45
World War I, 32
World War II, 39, 41
Wright, Thomas, 45
Wright, Wallace, 45
Wrightwood Avenue, 19, 25, 38
Wrigley Building, 20
Wronkiewicz, Joseph, 45
Wurbia, Anita, 60
Wurbia, John, 60

Y

Yates, Joseph F., 45
Yates, Sidney R., 12
Young Ladies Sodality, 46, 49
Youngs People's Club, 38, 40, 46

Z

Zabrovitz, Casimir, 45
Zale, Tony, 46
Zambrovitz, C. B., 45
Zentschel, Robert, 45
Ziak, Geraldine Sister, 31